An Exceptional Journey

On Saturday, August 28, 2004, the big conference room at the Methodist Home for Children started filling up with people gathering to celebrate the fiftieth wedding anniversary of Billy and Peggy Griffin. The couple's children, Brenda and Bruce, wanted it to be exciting for all of the people who had shared in their parents' lives. There was a buffet of barbecue and lots of good country dishes, and everything was informal—just the way Billy and Peggy wanted it.

More than one hundred of their friends and family members came to help them celebrate this special day. There were orphanage brothers and sisters, biological siblings, coworkers, children, and grandchildren all in one room. A special table held hundreds of congratulatory cards and letters. Old pictures of Billy and Peggy were displayed on every table and on big boards. The guests played games and read old letters and made fun of the things Billy and Peggy had chosen to keep over the years.

Brenda read notes from family members and a few tears were shed as everyone remembered some very happy times—and some not so happy. Guests were interviewed for a video about how they felt about the honored couple. Many used words like "committed" and "devoted" to describe the couple. Some made comments like "they were meant to be together" and "they have truly become one." It was hard not to notice a common theme: Billy and Peggy were unique. They had shared a lifetime of joy and sorrow, much like all devoted couples. However, there was a distinct difference. This couple began their journey together while living in an orphanage. As fate would have it they found each other in a very special way and in a very special place.

Their journey would have been much different without the many people who cared about them and wanted them to have full and productive lives. Billy and Peggy praise God, today and always, for giving them each other and allowing them to learn and grow together in their faith and their love for one another.

They both first learned about Christ as children in the Methodist Orphanage. Christian teachings were very much a part of the life there, and Billy and Peggy are grateful for those teachings. It is part of who they are today.

Peggy

My name is Peggy Patton Griffin. I was born in Franklin County, North Carolina, to Myrtle Collier Patton and Richard Patton on June 9, 1935. I was their fifth child, born after my brothers, K.C., Orlando, and Jack, and my sister, Rubye; my younger sister, Ann, was born two years after I was. We were six children in a family already struggling with extreme poverty, and my mother gave birth to another baby boy named Billy soon after my father's passing.

I recall little of the years before I turned five. The only real memory I have is of the night my father passed away. He was forty-one years old and suffered a fatal heart attack. My younger sister and I were sitting on his knees when he said he didn't feel well and needed to lie down. I remember he was very sick, vomiting and coughing up blood. My mother was frantic and crying. When Dad took his last breath she screamed loudly. I was too young to know that night would change my life forever.

I have always enjoyed talking about my life and am fascinated by people's interest in what happened to me. My life seems normal to me since it's the only one I've ever known. People have told me I should write a book about my life; I found it amusing and gave little thought to doing it. However, I'm now seventy-six years old, and at this age I feel I might have something to tell.

At least putting pen to paper will record for history's sake a life that has not been unusual but perhaps a little different from most people's journeys.

Billy

My name is William Ray Griffin, Jr., but most people call me Billy. I was born in Durham, North Carolina, to Sybil Barnes Griffin and William Ray Griffin, Sr. on August 4, 1934. I was their second child, born two years after my sister, Pauline. Two brothers, Donald Keith and John Phillip were born after me. Donald recently passed away. We were an average family struggling to live in the Depression and keep food on the table.

On the night of April 3, 1945, I was eleven years old and was playing catch with my father in the yard of our home. We frequently enjoyed this time together, just before we settled in for the night. When we were through, I went to bed as usual. In the morning I awoke to the most horrible news I could imagine: my father had passed away at the age of thirty-seven from a heart attack. I refused to accept the news. I felt it was all a mistake. But I was a wrong. He was gone, and my life had changed forever.

As sad as I was at that time, I now enjoy telling the stories of what happened to me after my father's death. I was old enough to know mine was not a normal life, but I embraced it with all the energy I had. Many people have told me I should write about my life but I've always felt too ordinary in many ways. I'm now seventy-seven years old, though, and for those who would like to know about me I am ready to share.

The Beginning

Billy

It was a warm, summer day in August 1946. My mother had taken my sister, my two brothers, and me to visit my grandmother in Cash Corner, North Carolina, located in Pamlico County. We were sitting in the Freewill Baptist Church, where my grandmother was a member. It was a tradition for each churchgoer, on his or her birthday, to contribute a penny for each year he or she had lived. Each time a person in the church had a birthday, a special celebration was held to recognize that person. Since I was not a member of the church I did not know they would recognize me. When the preacher asked if there were any birthdays to celebrate, my grandmother turned to me and said "Billy, today is your special day". She proceeded to open her purse and began taking out pennies. I had no idea why she was getting the pennies out and I asked her "Grandmother, why are you taking out the pennies?" She replied "Today, we will donate eleven pennies to the church in your honor". I was so proud and especially when she told me I could put the pennies in the jar that was on the table in front of the church. I proudly walked to the front of the church and one by one put the pennies in the jar. After I had placed the pennies in the jar the congregation sang Happy Birthday to me. It was a very special birthday.

After several days of visiting my grandmother and grandfather as well as other relatives in the area, my mother, my sister, my brother, and I left to return to our home in Durham. At least that was where I thought we would go. Instead we went to our uncle's tobacco farm in Pitt County. My brother Donald and I would spend three weeks there, helping on the farm. It was a fun time, and I learned a lesson about hard work that would help me in my teen years. My brother and I got to ride on the tractor, play with the pets, and go swimming in the pond, and we had three delicious country meals a day. There were no air conditioners or television; we listened to the radio for entertainment.

There was always a lot of work to be done on my uncle's farm. On this first day we were at the farm, Uncle Joe woke us up early and told us, "get dressed and come downstairs for breakfast". "We need to go to the fields to help out with the work". Granny was already cooking breakfast and the fat back and eggs smelled so good. We ate a big breakfast that would probably last us at least until noon. After breakfast, we rode on the farm wagon to the fields we would be working that day. We picked tobacco from the stalks and loaded it on the wagon and took the load back to the tobacco barns. Uncle Joe said to me, "Billy, you can help hand the tobacco to the person tying the tobacco on to the tobacco sticks". It was fascinating to watch the person tying go so fast putting the tobacco on the stick. When it was full, the stick was placed into the barn to be cured. It was a long day but my brother Donald and I really enjoyed relaxing with the grown ups after we finished a day's work. We would sit amongst the big oak trees and talk. Donald and I would mostly listen and we learned a few things from the older people. They accepted us as part of the work team and we felt really grownup after this experience. Each subsequent day we went through the same routine.

Donald and I had worked hard for three solid weeks. We had enjoyed our visits with our cousins and Uncle Joe. It was now time for us to leave and return to Durham because school was about to start and we had to be ready. We packed up and walked on to the big front porch of our uncle's home. We were sad to be leaving but happy to be going home. Uncle Joe came out to the porch and said, "boys you have done a very good job and I am proud of you." He then handed us $25.00 to share. To us, that was a lot of money and we were delighted to receive it. We were taken to the local bus station where we boarded a bus going back to Durham.

A few days later, on Monday, September 2, 1946—Labor Day—my mother put our clothes into a suitcase and drove Donald and me to our new home: the Methodist Orphanage in Raleigh, North Carolina, the place where my father had been raised. My younger brother, Johnny, who was six, would live with my grandmother, and our sister would stay with my mother as she was too old to be admitted to the orphanage. After my father's death, my mother found herself with four children to support and no work experience. She had to find a way to have her children taken care of.

Billy's Mom and Dad

I was devastated to leave the friends I had grown up with. I felt life would never be the same and I would be unhappy forever.

Peggy

My mother was forty years old and pregnant with my youngest brother when my father passed away. Shortly after that, a local Methodist minister visited and advised her that some of her children should be placed in an orphanage, where they could be cared for properly. There were seven of us; I have been told my mother lost several children before I was born. I remember seeing my mother's bible with names of children that had passed away. I can't remember but three of the names but I have been told my mother gave birth to at least ten children in all. The three names I remember seeing written in the bible are Patty Lou, Henry Tucker and William Douglas. I do not recall seeing the date or time of their death, or what they died from. I have no knowledge of where her bible is now.

Of the seven children my mother had left to take care of, four of the younger ones would go to the orphanage. My older sister, who was thirteen years old at the time, one older brother, and my youngest brother, when he was born, would remain with my mother.

Things happened so fast it became a blur. Our family was going to be separated; we would never be together again. I feel no sadness about this because now I know it was the best thing for all of us. However, I do regret not having a close relationship with my siblings throughout my life.

On July 5, 1941 my older sister, Rubye, told us to wash up because company was coming. I washed myself and put on a clean dress and shoes. We had to sit on the porch because we would get dirty if we played in the yard. Pretty soon we saw a cloud of dust down the dirt road leading to our house. We hardly ever saw a car where we lived and it seemed strange that someone would be visiting us.

Peggy as a young girl

The Beginning

"Someone's coming!" I yelled out to my mother, my older sister and my brother Jack who were inside the house. They all came out on the porch to greet the guest. The car pulled up and a kind-looking, grayed-haired man stepped out, and then went inside with my mother. We could hear them talking but did not know what they were discussing. We waited on the porch until my mother came out of the house and said to us; "you will be going with the nice man". We were confused and frightened and I am sure my brothers must have put up some serious objections because they were crying. I did not know why they were crying but I knew it was a sad time for them. They were old enough to know they did not like what was about to happen. My mother told us she loved us and she would see us soon. The nice man put his arm around me and said "you are going to be fine, don't worry, you are safe with me". I seem to remember my older sister crying as she left the porch and went into the house. I don't remember if we took anything with us because we didn't have much of anything to take anyway.

Peggy is in the front row, third from left.

The Baby Cottage

Peggy

We arrived at 1001 Glenwood Avenue in Raleigh and drove up a long hill lined with beautiful oak trees and lots of big buildings. We were taken to the infirmary—the first stop for all new arrivals at the Methodist Orphanage. The infirmary was a large building on the back of the campus. Two sleeping porches were on the top floor with several beds on each porch.

A nurse named Miss Fogleman came out to greet us in a starched, white uniform. She was a little short lady with pretty blue eyes. Her hair was white as snow and she had a sweet expression on her face. Another lady we called Stick Watson came out to greet us with Miss Fogleman. She was a very skinny lady with big blue eyes and really white teeth. She had been raised in the orphanage and after graduating accepted a paying job working in the infirmary with the nurse. She was a gentle lady who genuinely cared about the children and we loved her. Miss Fogleman said to us, "You'll stay with us for a while and then you'll go live with other children. You will be fine and well taken care of."

My memory is rather vague on how long we stayed in the infirmary. Eventually my sister and I were taken to the Baby Cottage, where the youngest children lived, and my two older brothers went to other buildings to live with boys their age. This separation was the first sad thing I experienced at my new home. I also didn't know where my little sister was for a number of days; eventually I learned she had gotten blood poisoning after stepping on a rusty nail and was at Duke Hospital in Durham.

At least thirty other children, both boys and girls, lived in the Baby Cottage with me. We slept in cribs with girls and boys right across from each other. I've often wondered how we fit into cribs at six years old. I guess they were special little beds designed just for our age and sizes.

A number of older girls helped take care of us little ones, and a matron who was in charge of the children lived in the building. We never saw the inside of her quarters. The matron wasted no time on getting us acclimated to our new environment. There was certainly no hugging or kissing, but there were a lot of rules. The big girls who took care of us told us to keep up with our tooth brush and wash our hands after using the bathroom, and not to talk after we went to bed. They repeated it to make sure we understood. I really didn't, but I nodded my head because I felt this was the right thing to do. I was scared and didn't know what they would do to me if I didn't respond the way they wanted me to. They were the authority; I recognized that the first day I arrived at the Baby Cottage.

We spent our days playing in a large room in the basement of the building, and on a pretty day we were taken to the playground next to the building. Nighttime was the worst. The girls put us in our little cribs and told us to be quiet and go to sleep. If we had to go to the bathroom during the night we could climb out and go by ourselves. We had to be as self-sufficient as possible.

Though I was in a strange place for the first time in my life, I don't remember crying, but I heard some other children crying softly during the night.

In the morning the big girls came in and told us to get dressed. They combed our hair and made sure we were dressed properly, and then we walked up a long, gravel hill to a big dining room to eat breakfast. This was where we ate all our meals—with over three hundred other

The Baby Cottage

children. There were little tables in the middle of the dining room just for us little people.

Before each meal a bell rang to let us know it was time for Daddy Barnes, the orphanage's superintendent, to say the blessing: "For these and all thy gifts of love, we give thee thanks and praise." Daddy Barnes was like a father to all of us. He was a tall man, about six foot five inches, with gray hair and very big feet that he rocked back and forth on when he prayed. He had a real gentleness about him; I never heard or saw him be harsh to any child. I felt safe with him and believed he would not let anything happen to me. I have great memories of him.

I don't remember whether the food was good or not, but I enjoyed having something to eat on a regular basis. We were encouraged to eat all of the food served to us, and we did. Breakfast usually consisted of cereal, eggs, milk, grits, and some bacon and toast. . There were times when we had green pea soup that was almost impossible to eat and we would think of creative ways to dispose of it. Quite often a child would try to pour their soup into another child's bowl when they were not looking. This type of behavior would usually result in some type of punishment for the child so it was not a frequent activity.

After we finished our meal we would walk back down the long, gravel road to our building to stay until the next meal. We played all day and would sometimes get in trouble without meaning to. Life was not too complicated but it wasn't easy either. When we broke the rules or did something we shouldn't have, the punishments were severe. Wetting our pants, which happened frequently among six-year-olds, carried a penalty most of us will never forget: the boys had to wear dresses and the girls had to wear little boy's suits. It was embarrassing and quickly taught us to hold it.

When we were overly aggressive while playing, the matron spanked us. A hard smack on the bottom or the face was not unusual, and we did whatever we could to avoid it. I quickly learned how to play with other children and to stay out of trouble.

While living in the Baby Cottage, I started school. I was in the first grade, which was a very happy time for me. I especially loved making music in front of everyone when we had special programs in the auditorium. We had a stick band, which was each pupil holding two special sticks and clanging them together in time with the music. One person had the special job of clanging two cymbals together; another played the triangle. I even did it once. I also led the band once as well. I was so proud.

Our first grade teacher, Miss Mary Ferree, was a true angel—sweet and soft spoken and really loved all children. She maintained strict discipline but always did it with kindness and understanding, and she made every day joyful and fun. If there was ever a real saint, she was one. In her class I felt love for the first time since entering the orphanage. Miss Mary lived on the campus with us, so we got to see her often. I believe God put her there to make sure we were always taken care of and no harm would come to us.

Grades one through six went to school in the morning while the older students did chores on the campus or the farm. Grades seven through twelve went to school in the afternoon. We also had two hours of supervised study hall each night. I hated leaving school each day to go back to my building. I so looked forward to the morning when I once again could be with Miss Mary.

My mother was allowed to visit, and she would usually come by bus on Saturday or Sunday. She would bring my baby brother with her. I don't remember whether I was happy or sad when I saw her; I only knew I was in a place where I had clean sheets to sleep on and food to eat. I don't think I felt abandoned or unloved by my mother. I knew I was never going to live with her again, but I looked forward to seeing her when she visited. But I can't really say I understood anything during that period of my life. I just know each day I lived at the orphanage made me more trusting, more independent, and more self-confident.

As I mentioned earlier, my mother came to see us whenever she could get a ride or money for a bus trip. At first she came at least once a month. When I turned eight or nine years old I enjoyed her visits because I liked playing with my baby brother. My mother was a poor country woman who dipped snuff and sometimes let it run down the corner of her mouth. This embarrassed me; I didn't like the other children to see it. Many people who knew her when she was a young woman have told me she was beautiful and always full of life. To me she was old and wrinkled, and that was when she was in her forties.

Sometimes an uncle or my older brother would bring her to see my sister and me. Many cars came up the long hill. When a particularly old car came up the hill, some of the children would yell out to me "Peggy Patton your people are coming". They understood status—strange for children living in an orphanage—and knew how poor we were. Some of them had relatives who sent them money or clothes. We had no one who could afford to give us anything.

In later years, after my older sister got married and my brothers had left the orphanage, my sister Rubye would send me a little money and visit me from time to time. On one occasion my mother sent me money to buy an evening gown for a music recital. This was a real sacrifice for her since she had no money to spare. All she had was tied up in her handkerchief. She had so little, she didn't need a purse. When we visited her in the summer I was always fascinated by that.

I have orphanage brothers and sisters who started the first grade with me and together we finished twelve grades and graduated from the Methodist Orphanage High School. These siblings are so important to me even today. We love each other as if we were biologically related. We see each other as often as we can and stay in touch almost constantly.

Atwater Building

Peggy

When I was eight years old I was moved from the Baby Cottage to the Atwater Building. The matron there was named Miss Tull, a tall, stern-looking woman with big, boney hands. She had long, black hair that she wore in a bun on the back of her neck. She had probably been a very beautiful woman when she was younger.

Almost immediately I developed a real dislike for Miss Tull and the feeling seemed to be mutual. Even at that young age I could sense when I was not favored by someone. Of course, being in an orphanage gave us all a sixth sense about such things. I guess you could call it a survival instinct—something I would learn a lot about in the coming years.

The Atwater Building had a basement with pigeonholes where we could keep our meager belongings. We slept upstairs in dormitories and stored our clothes just outside of the matron's living quarters, which consisted of a bedroom, a bath, and a small kitchen. The building also had a large front porch where we frequently sat and played or just talked. I vividly remember Miss Tull crocheting small pieces to put together and make a bedspread. It took her at least a year to get enough pieces.

Sometimes I got into hair-pulling fights with other girls. This was a rather frequent occurrence because living in such close quarters is not always easy. I can truthfully say I never started a fight, but I didn't let anyone take advantage of me, and regardless of who did start it I always got blamed. More than once Miss Tull slapped me across the face with her boney knuckles, but this physical punishment didn't hurt me the most. The verbal abuse did. That's stayed with me all of my life.

On one occasion Miss Tull told my sister and me we had come from nothing and would go back to nothing. This was hard to take. Our family was poor—every summer when we went to visit our mother she was living in a different tenant house, anywhere she could work as a share cropper—but we never thought we were less than other people until it was brought to our attention in such a cruel manner. One thing's for certain: it made me tougher and able to deal with the years I had left at the orphanage. I was determined to make something of myself and prove Miss Tull wrong.

I don't believe Miss Tull was an evil person. She had raised a family of her own and was spending her later years looking after other children who were not hers. It was probably not how she wanted to spend her years of retirement but times were tough and she had to do whatever she could to survive. It's no wonder she got frustrated at times and took it out on the children.

We didn't have assigned duties in the Atwater Building. We did have chores to do, like picking up sticks, raking leaves, and cleaning up the building. I liked raking because we could dive into the leaves once we got the pile big enough. Picking up sticks was no fun and I still don't like it today.

I always tried to do what I was told because I didn't like being punished or spanked. I do recall one really nice thing Miss Tull did for me. The matrons were able to get fresh cream from the milk in the dining room. We had our own dairy, so fresh milk was always available. She would put it into a quart jar and get me to shake it until it turned to butter. She would then give me a glass of cold buttermilk to drink. It was delicious. I'm sure the butter was too, but I never got to taste it. The only people fortunate enough to have any of the good stuff like that were Miss Tull and her favorite orphanage girl, who lived in a private room upstairs with another girl who was very small for her age. She spent

Atwater Building

hours with Miss Tull, eating snacks in the little kitchen while the rest of us raked leaves and picked up sticks. She never had to work at a really hard job. She was assigned to the business office, where she learned typing and other skills. I can't remember that we resented her much; we just accepted that she was special. She was a kind girl and never caused any trouble for anyone.

Every night after supper we would play scrub. Someone would pitch a handmade sock ball and someone else would hit it with her hand and run bases, the same as in traditional baseball games. To get a runner out, the opponent could hit her with the ball. I could make a good sock ball—I rolled it hard and tied it real tight. This was a valuable toy, and I would guard it with my life. I experienced many a hair-pulling fight to protect what was mine, and I must say I usually won.

The children who didn't like playing outside would play paper dolls, pick up sticks, or jack rocks. I remember one girl who made her own clothes for her paper dolls. She would draw them and then cut them out. She was very talented. One favorite game almost everyone played at one time or another was penny show. We would look for the prettiest pieces of broken glass, wild flowers, smooth rocks, and anything we could use to make the best penny show. We would find a smooth plot of earth and clean it with the palms of our hands. Then we would build a design from the materials we had collected and cover it with a rag, then cover that with dirt. We would then start another design on top of that until we had at least five designs to uncover.

When it was all set, we hollered, "Come to a penny show!" A crowd would gather and we would start the show by scraping the dirt off of the first design. Everyone sighed in appreciation. We continued until we reached the last design—the finale and the best design of all. Everyone would clap when we scraped the dirt off and revealed it.

In the Atwater Building I experienced some of the worst times while living at the orphanage. Once I was really sick; I told Miss Tull I hurt and felt so bad. She told me to quit complaining and go to the infirmary. She also told me if I continued to complain I would be punished.

The nurse at the infirmary was very nice but said I didn't have a temperature, so I went back to my building. I continued to feel pain all over my body, and all I could do was lie on the benches in the basement and sleep. My muscles ached and I felt sick to my stomach. I grew sicker every day and there was nothing I could do to make me feel better. I didn't want to tell Miss Tull because I knew she didn't believe me, but I was desperate and wanted so much to get well. So I told her, and again she sent me to the infirmary with another promise of punishment for complaining. The nurse again said I didn't appear to be sick, but she let me lie down for a while. When she took my temperature again later, it registered 104 and she became very concerned. She called the doctor to come see me.

When he got there, he examined me and said I had the flu. I was sick enough to be in the infirmary for at least a week. I will never forget that. To this day I have a hard time telling anyone when I'm sick or hurting.

* * *

I loved the big swings on the playground behind the Atwater Building. There were four of them on a tall, metal frame. I could stand on a swing and go so high I could loop the top pole.

We played jump board almost daily in the summertime. We would find a small hill and place a six-by-twelve inch board on it. One person would stand on each end, and then one of them would jump, throwing the other high into the air. This was very dangerous, but I can't remember any child being hurt while playing this game—we were really good at it. We also had a swimming pool, a skating rink, and outdoor one-lane bowling alley, and tennis courts on the campus. We could use them at scheduled times, and we took full advantages. In the summer we swam every day; there was a little wading pool for the very young children and a diving board in the big part. I loved to dive and got quite good at doing the jackknife and flips. My brother was a wonderful diver as well.

Another big part of our daily lives was religious education. We went to chapel every Sunday night and church every Sunday, and we had Sunday school. I will always remember this part of my life—and be grateful for it.

Atwater Building

When I was eleven years old, a new group of children came to live at the orphanage. I saw them go into the infirmary when I was playing on the playground, which was right across from it. I remember one of the boys vividly: he was cute and had curly hair, and he carried a trombone. I remember wondering how long that horn would last once he was assigned to the Page Building with thirty other boys who had probably never seen such a beautiful instrument. This observation and this boy would be very important to me in the months and years to come.

Before The Orphanage

Billy

When my father was nine years old, his mother gave birth to his sister, Maude, and died shortly thereafter. In addition to his newborn sister, he had one brother, Hugh, and three sisters, Kathleen, Della Lee, and Georgia. Now his father had six children to support with no wife beside him. He turned to the Methodist Church in Washington, North Carolina, for help.

Arrangements were made for the children to be placed in the Methodist Orphanage in Raleigh. They arrived there in 1917 and would stay until they graduated from high school. My father, William Ray Griffin, Sr., left the orphanage in 1926. He went to live in Durham, where he worked for American Tobacco Company, as did Della Lee.

Soon after leaving the orphanage, my father met my mother and they were married in 1930. They started a family right away; my sister, Pauline, was born on December 16, 1932. My mother gave birth to me on August 4, 1934. We weren't rich, but we were a family.

I can remember eating a lot of navy beans with Worcestershire sauce poured over them. It seemed like we had them almost every night. I can also remember wearing clothes that were a little too big for me so they would last longer. My dad worked hard to provide for us, and we felt safe and secure.

An Exceptional Journey

On August 5, 1940—the day after my birthday—I was at a local hospital awaiting tonsil surgery. I had a roommate, a young girl who was having the same surgery as me. I remember the doctor asking who wanted to go first. I wanted to put it off as long as possible, so I quickly answered, "Girls first." When my turn came, the doctor put a cloth over my nose and dropped ether onto it to put me to sleep.

When I awoke from the surgery my dad was standing beside my bed with a vanilla milkshake and a straw. This would be the extent of my nourishment for the next few days. My mother was bedridden with some pregnancy issues, so she was unable to be with me. She gave birth to my brother, John, three days after I was released and three days later they came home. My mother found me sick, and that night I was rushed back to the hospital with a ruptured appendix. The doctors told my mother I probably would not live through the night due to complications from a ruptured appendix. I struggled for several days to live.

Lying in a bed in a ward with other children, I waited for visiting time to begin. There were six beds and a door separating us from the waiting room. I heard my father cough, and I knew he was there, waiting to see me. When the door opened, he was the first person I saw. He was holding a vanilla milkshake with a straw. I was so excited.

I remember another time when something very exciting happened to me—but this time it was a very happy thing. Movie theaters were very popular back then, since television had not yet been introduced; you could see a feature film and usually a news reel before the movie began.

You could also, if you were lucky, get to see a movie star. A number of them visited theaters to promote their films. One of the most well-known Western stars at the time was Roy Rogers, known as the King of the Cowboys. My dad took me to the Rialto Theater once when Roy was promoting his new picture with his horse, Trigger. After the screening my dad and I went to the lobby. He held me in his arms and when Roy came in; he walked up to us, took me from my dad, held me and talked to me. What a moment! It's stayed with me for a lifetime.

I also remember a Christmas parade in Durham. This was during the war years after the bombing of Pearl Harbor, and members of the armed forces were supposed to be there. The Orange Crush Bottling Company sponsored a float and had young children representing the four branches of the armed services: the Army, Air Force, Marines, and Navy. They chose me to represent the Navy and I dressed up in my very own Navy suit. After the parade was over, each of us received a six-pack of Orange Crush drinks. Another day I've never forgotten.

* * *

My first memory of the Methodist Orphanage takes me back to a beautiful spring Sunday in 1944. My father was there for the annual Easter Reunion of the Methodist Orphanage Alumni Association. A baseball game was in progress on the field behind the Page Building and he was playing; when he got up to bat, he called me to come and stand beside him. He told me to run to first base after he hit the ball. Sure enough, he hit it, and I began to run. I arrived safe. I was nine years old at the time, and I've never forgotten this experience.

A year later almost to the day, I waited anxiously for my father to come home from work. We always did something fun together, and that night we played baseball in the backyard while my mother and sister got supper ready. I loved throwing the ball around with him—but I enjoyed doing everything with him. When supper was ready we all ate together, and later went to bed. Everything in my life was perfect—at least so I thought.

During the night I woke up and heard some activity downstairs, but I soon fell right back to sleep. In the morning our cousin, Thelma, who was living with us at that time, came into our room and informed my brother and me that our father had a massive heart attack and died during the night. He was only thirty-seven years old. Suddenly my world was turned up side down and I thought life would never be the same again. The next day I got on my bicycle and rode to the funeral home; I wanted to see my father. As fate would have it my bike's chain came off and I had to turn around and go back home, walking the bicycle the entire way. Then it started to rain.

Eventually I got to the funeral home for my father's service and to the grave site for his burial. This was a traumatic experience for me; to this day I find it difficult to go to funerals.

An Exceptional Journey

After the death of my father, my uncle—the husband of my father's sister—befriended me. He had no children of his own, but he did have season tickets to the local baseball team's home games. Many times he telephoned my mother and told her he would pick me up for a game. When there were no games in the summer, I walked to the ballpark to learn the game from the players. They let me in their practice and I would play catch, shag balls, run, and talk. I had a lot of fun with the team members.

I remember when I was nine years old the boys in our neighborhood would walk to the Durham Athletic Park, where the movie *Bull Durham* was filmed, and look through the holes in the fences to watch the game. We were known as the knotholers. Eventually a local businessman started a program known as The Knothole Gang and got us admitted to all the games free of charge. This eventually led to my learning and enjoying the game of baseball.

Billy, before going to the orphanage.

McGee Building

Peggy

I was eleven years old when I was moved to the McGee Building to live with other girls my age. This building was named after a very generous and kind doctor who served the children of the orphanage. As in the other buildings, we had a matron: Miss Lizzie. She was so afraid of thunderstorms, whenever one hit, she would ask one of the children to sleep with her until it passed. I was happy I was never chosen for this experience—I did not want to sleep with an old woman.

Miss Lizzie had her private living quarters. She'd never married, so having a place to live and lots of little girls to take care of was just perfect for her. She didn't have favorites amongst us; she treated us all alike. Two older girls did live upstairs because they were assigned to help Miss Lizzie take care of the thirty young girls who lived in the building, but other than that they seemed to get no preferential treatment.

Miss Lizzie loved flowers, particularly African violets. She named all of her flowers and loved them so much. She was as gentle with her flowers as she was with the children. She was much less quick to judge than our previous matron and rarely laid a hand on any child.

She loved to sew but had difficulty threading the needles because of her poor eyesight, so she would ask one of the girls do it for her.

At that age we were assigned to work in the dining room, laundry room, sewing room, kitchen, or to do housework. A few were fortunate enough to work in the administrative office; they were, in our opinions, the chosen ones. I was never one of them. But I was a good worker and spent several years serving food. I also worked in the laundry. I learned to iron shirts with starched collars without a wrinkle. If there was one, the shirt went back into the starch pot and I started all over again. Thankfully this didn't happen too often.

The basement still served as our primary home when we weren't sleeping and again we had pigeonholes to keep our meager belongings: toothpaste, toothbrushes, and maybe some lotion if we had someone to give it to us. We also kept our socks in the pigeonholes and washed them and our underpants by hand. Afterward we would hang them on the exposed pipes in the basement to dry. A coal furnace provided heat and hot water ran through the pipes so they stayed hot most of the time.

We were somewhat more independent at this age. We were able to select our own clothes when we went shopping with money donated by members of the Methodist Churches. We received $50 in the spring and the same in the winter for several years. Eventually it went up to $75 and that allowed us to buy a little more. We shopped at Hudson Belk Store in downtown Raleigh on requisition. The people who worked there were always very kind and respectful of us, and we loved to shop there.

Each child living at the orphanage had a sponsor from a Methodist Church. My sponsor was the Women's Society of Christian Service in Fuquay Springs, North Carolina. They were so good to me, and I was able to visit with them on a number of occasions. They invited me to their homes and served me delicious meals, usually fried chicken and fresh vegetables with good, creamy potatoes. It felt good to be special to someone.

The women in the church also sent me Christmas and birthday gifts. One Christmas I received my very first doll with a little bed. Before I opened it, I kept hearing the girls in the building whispering about it; they must have seen it before it was put under the tree. On Christmas morning I got the doll and I could not have been happier. It was the most beautiful doll I had ever seen.

McGee Building

My mother came to see me shortly after that and told me she would take the doll home for me. I never saw it again. I hope some of my nieces enjoyed playing with it. I understand why my mother did such a thing, since she had no money to buy gifts for her grandchildren and she knew I would receive other gifts.

* * *

When I turned twelve years old I was given permission to go to Green's Service Store by myself, at the foot of the long hill. Girls also usually got bras at that age whether or not they wanted or needed them. It was a growing-up period. It was around that time I first talked back to a matron. Miss Lizzie told me to rake a rock garden next to the McGee Building, but it was very cold outside. After attempting to complete the job, I suddenly thought to myself that I had a brain and I was going to use it. I wasn't going to rake that rock garden in freezing weather. I put my rake down and went inside the building, where it was warm.

When Miss Lizzie saw me she asked, "Why are you not raking the rock garden?"

I replied in my most defiant voice, "I'm not going to do it. It's too cold." She punished me. I had to stay in the building for two weekends. But I did not rake the garden.

At other times my defiance almost got me in serious trouble. In the McGee Building the other girls and I entertained ourselves by swinging on the exposed pipes in the basement. There was little activity for us, especially in the winter months when it was too cold to play outside. Swinging on the pipes satisfied our need for physical activity.

After doing it for a while, I developed a callous on my hand, and it hurt a lot. It looked like a small blister but it was hard instead of soft. I was hesitant to go to the infirmary because it looked hardly worth treating, but finally it hurt too much, and I went. I showed my hand to the nurse and she said it was nothing but a superficial wound caused by the constant rubbing on the pipes. Then she told me not to come to the infirmary unless something was really hurting.

I couldn't believe she was denying my illness a second time. In my most defiant voice, I said, "I will not come back to the infirmary even if I am dying." I was a feisty twelve-year-old, and I meant every word of it.

I went back to my building with my hand hurting so bad I could hardly stand it. I told my younger sister about it and she rubbed it to try to make it better. But it got worse and worse, and my hand swelled and turned red. One day, soon after my visit to the infirmary, I was raking the yard with a number of other girls. I couldn't hold the rake because my hand was so swollen. I tried to do it with one hand but it was difficult to maneuver.

My mother came to visit and came into the yard where I was working. She noticed I was having difficulty holding the rake and asked me what was wrong. I told her the story and she became so angry. She approached the matron and then took me back to the infirmary, where I was diagnosed with severe blood poisoning. I spent more than two weeks in the hospital. I remember holding my hand in a tub for a long time. The nurse would come in and check it often to make sure the infection hadn't spread.

I was too young to realize the seriousness of blood poisoning, but this wasn't the first experience I'd had with it. My sister had also been diagnosed with it soon after coming to the orphanage, and she'd spent a number of weeks in the hospital. However, I hadn't even understood where she was, much less that she was so sick. I was only six at the time.

This whole episode taught me an important lesson: there are consequences to being stubborn and arrogant. Though I didn't want to return to the infirmary out of spite, I should have. It might have saved me a lot of pain in the long run.

I stayed in the McGee Building for about three years. I worked in the laundry and the dining room. I also had a stint as a house girl. In the laundry, I got to be real good at ironing and learned to work the big presser, of which I was very proud. The matron in charge of the laundry liked me. She was a beautiful lady and the wife of the orphanage's business manager. She would let me and others iron her many handkerchiefs. They had beautiful, bright flower designs, and we just loved ironing them for her. She stood up for me one time when one of the other girls accused me of taking some fudge from her. Truth was her sister had given it to me. The matron was a fair lady and treated us well if we did our jobs like we were supposed to and treated her with respect.

In the dining room, I set up for all three meals and then waited on the tables when all of the 300 children and our matrons came to eat. The dining room matron immediately disliked me because I was sitting at her table for lunch and took some chocolate pudding before she took her serving. I know it was rude, but I just wasn't thinking. Instead of correcting me she told everyone I was no longer allowed to sit at her table. This embarrassed me and hurt my feelings. I began to get a complex that I was just not a likable person. I rebelled; I had to let people know they couldn't take advantage of me, and that meant matrons as well as other children. I stayed away from the dining room for a few days.

The matron, unaware that I still was able to sneak food out of the kitchen when I wanted it, asked me why I refused to eat. I responded in a sassy way that it was because she thought she was too good for me to eat at her table. She slapped me on the face so hard it knocked me off my feet. I was headstrong, and the slap didn't mean much to me, but having to wash windows on a Saturday or work on the vegetable porch shelling peas was much harder. This was my punishment for being arrogant.

* * *

Several older girls and I moved into the actual dining room to live so we could serve an early breakfast for the boys when they returned from milking cows on the orphanage's farm. We slept two to a room instead of the usual eight or ten, and it was wonderful. I loved having a dresser with vanity lamps.

I turned fourteen while living in the dining room, and so many things were changing in my life. It was a happy time for me, but that was temporary, as soon I had to move back to the basement of the McGee Building. The matron and orphanage staff tried to work with me to make the adjustment easy, but I was displeased and I let them all know. They gave me a room upstairs with another girl, but that didn't last long. We were told we had to keep the room neat and make up our beds every day. My roommate was sloppy and refused to keep her part of the room neat. Because we had failed to do what we had been asked to do, we were moved back to the basement with the other girls. I hated it.

* * *

My favorite activity as I got older was playing basketball and watching the older girls play in front of everyone in our gymnasium. They looked so cool in their maroon and white uniforms, and I wanted to be just like them. Sports were a big part of my life. I made the team—the Red Raiders—quickly and had the opportunity to play with some of the most athletic girls, like Martha, Sarah, Lucille, Virginia, and others. We weren't the best in the conference, but we sure tried hard. Life couldn't have been any better. I even had a boyfriend—a nice, young man named Dennis who played football and was very athletic. I liked having a boyfriend, and I thought it would last but it didn't. We were both so young, and we soon decided there were other boys and girls for us to get to know. Thus ended my first romance.

Basketball was such an important part of my life while living at the orphanage. I had always been fairly athletic and playing basketball was so much fun. I loved wearing the *MO uniform* and keeping my sneakers as white as they could be. I played guard, but the position was different from what it is today. I couldn't shoot the basketball; I just played defensively and got little credit since I was not able to score points. I could only dribble twice before passing the ball and played only one end of the court. I guess I was pretty feisty because I got the ball from the other team more than I should have. They were bigger, but I was faster.

I loved it when Billy refereed games. I was proud he was my boyfriend and knew how to call the fouls and keep the game fair. One time I turned my ankle and he had to lift me up and carry me off the court. Everyone clapped. In my senior year I received a trophy for being the most outstanding player. I was so proud.

McGee Building

Playing sports at the orphanage consumed much of my time. I loved skating around the rink with my clip-on skates. If I failed to tie them tight enough I would take a tumble and skin my knees, and risk even breaking an arm or a leg. None of us ever seemed to worry about getting hurt, though. We were having too much fun.

On top of sports and dating, I still had to keep up with my chores as well. I continued serving in the dining room and the laundry; these two jobs, along with kitchen duty, were considered the hardest. I was a good worker, and several matrons asked for me to work for them—though some asked for me *not* to be assigned to them. I guess feistiness wasn't the most desirable trait, though some of the matrons didn't mind as long as I was respectful to them.

One time while working in the dining room I became very ill. I was just finishing setting up my assigned tables when I felt nauseated. I told the matron I couldn't finish my tables. She told me to try and I did, then ran outside and vomited. Several matrons were standing on the porch talking and they immediately came to my aid. They made arrangements for someone to take me to the infirmary.

As soon as I arrived the nurse called a cab to take me to the hospital. I was diagnosed with appendicitis and went into an operating room immediately. I spent a week in the hospital, and then returned to the orphanage as good as new. My boyfriend and my friends were glad to see me back home.

High school at the orphanage was like most high schools, though we had much smaller classes—an average of twenty-five students in each and sometimes less than that. Our teachers were excellent, compassionate and skilled at dealing with young people in an unusual situation. We had our own athletic program, and after basketball cheerleading was my next favorite thing to do. I loved cheering for the teams and wearing the cute uniform, which included a sweater with a big *MO* on the front.

I was fifteen when a boy named Billy asked another girl to ask me if he could walk me to my building after chapel. I was shocked he had even noticed me, much less wanted to walk me to my building. I said yes. He had just broken up with one of the cutest and most beautiful girls on campus and I knew I could not measure up to her. But what the heck? I would take a chance.

That night I fell in love. I felt that God had surely put Billy and me together for a reason, and my life seemed to be overflowing with joy and happiness. Everything was just perfect except for one thing: my mother had taken my younger sister, Ann, out of the orphanage to live with her. She'd also taken my brothers some time earlier. I missed them and felt totally detached from my biological family. However, I now had Billy and nothing else seemed to matter. I would be happy forever for as long as I could share my life with him.

Unfortunately, not all our times together were so happy. In 1950 the Methodist Orphanage High School offered class rings to those who could afford to purchase them. Most students were able to get them either as gifts or by paying for them with money from relatives or friends. Billy paid for his ring with money he earned doing a morning paper route. He was so proud of that ring and wore it all the time.

One night just before a basketball game he let me hold the ring. He put it on my finger. I dropped the ring into the deep snow on the ground. We immediately dug through the snow and leaves but couldn't find it. I was sick and heartbroken that I had lost the ring he loved so much. I felt certain he would hate me and wouldn't want to be my boyfriend anymore. He told me not to worry, maybe it would show up. But it never did. I would catch him every now and then rubbing his finger and I knew he was missing his ring.

Billy was the most forgiving person, and I believe he loved me more than the ring because we soon stopped talking about it. Twenty years later we received word from the staff at the orphanage that someone had found a ring with Billy's initials inside in the area where we had lost it. The stone was missing but the ring was fine. We still have the ring with a new stone. It's a reminder that love is stronger than things and we can overcome sadness and disappointment when we have someone special to share our lives with.

Billy graduated before me, in 1952, and I was so sad. I prayed he wouldn't forget me when he left the orphanage. It seemed like my lifeline was broken and life would never be the same. That's the way it is when you're young, yet life goes on and more beautiful things happen to you when you least expect it.

When I was a senior, I was chosen by popular vote to be an attendant in the annual May Court. I was surprised, as I had never considered myself a beautiful girl. I had always been in awe of the girls in the May Court, with their pretty gowns and handsome escorts. I remember the very first May Day celebration we had. The May Queen was chosen from the senior class and she was the most gorgeous girl I had ever seen. When she put on that white gown, with her black hair and flawless complexion, she looked like a movie star and I thought to myself, *I wish I could be half as pretty as she is*.

I couldn't wait to tell Billy I would be an attendant. He was happy for me, but I don't think he was too thrilled about my having an escort—even though he had been an escort on at least two occasions. He was even May King his senior year, and that hadn't been easy for me to see either. May Day was a happy time for me regardless, and I often look at the pictures from that day and still ask myself how I could have been picked when there were so many other pretty girls.

Burwell Building

Peggy

In the eleventh and twelfth grades, girls were assigned to live in the Burwell Building. I moved there when I was fifteen years old and a sophomore, and stayed until I graduated.

I have vivid memories of living in the Burwell Building. I felt so blessed to live in such a beautiful place. My first roommate was named Lucille and she was one of the sweetest girls at the orphanage. She was older than I was and in a higher grade, but she treated me with kindness and welcomed me to her room.

Burwell was furnished with beautiful antiques and had parquet floors. The living room had a rug imported from Spain and a baby grand piano. Some of the girls could play, and on many nights after supper we would stand around and sing. We played records on an old player some kind person had donated and danced. It was so much fun.

My happiest times while living in the Burwell Building were the weekends, when I could see Billy. We would sit in the living room with a number of other couples and steal kisses when the matron wasn't looking. After our two-hour visit ended, Billy and the other boys would go to the Milky Way, a store just off campus, and buy us milkshakes and ham and cheese sandwiches. The matron in our building would allow them to bring the food back to us. They had to leave as soon as they delivered the food.

I thought I was truly in heaven and life could not have been any better for me. Having a boyfriend like Billy was so special; he made me feel cherished. I had never felt that way before, and my self-esteem soared.

On one occasion we broke up for a short period—a week or two at most. Then I asked the matron if I could call Billy on the telephone. It was after nine o'clock p.m. and we weren't permitted to make calls at such a late hour.

I begged, "Please let me call him. I can't sleep and I feel like I'm going to die if I don't talk to him."

She replied, "No, Peggy, you know the rules. You can talk to him in the morning."

I told her if I couldn't talk to him I would leave the orphanage. I didn't want to stay if I couldn't talk to him. I went to my room and told my roommate I was leaving. Some of the other girls were there, and they just laughed because they knew I had no place to go.

I walked out the front door and down the long hill to the bottom of the road. I went to the end of the hill where the superintendent lived. He met me at the door and invited me in. The matron had called him to alert him I was on my way.

He asked me to sit down. I told him I was leaving and needed to borrow money for a bus ticket. He said he would help me. I began to feel frightened that he would actually let me leave.

"You need to date other boys and get to know other people," he said.

"I don't want to date other boys. I love Billy," I told him.

"You're young and it's wrong to tie yourself to just one boy."

"I love him and I will never love anyone else," I said.

"OK," he said. "If you're determined to leave, we need to go."

I was getting more nervous by the minute. We got into his car and started to drive. He asked me if I would like a chocolate milkshake. I said I would love one. We stopped by a little drive-in, then continued to drive and ended up in front of the Burwell Building.

He said, "Peggy, you know you don't want to leave the only home you've ever known." "This will pass and you'll be happy again, I promise."

When I walked into the building, some of the girls laughed at me, but one was compassionate and told me not to worry. She said I'd be able to talk to Billy in the morning and everything would be OK. She was right—the next day Billy and I made up, and we never broke up again.

* * *

The boys on our orphanage campus were allowed to do small jobs to make money. Billy delivered morning papers for the local newspaper and also cut grass for some local residents. This gave him spending money. With the money he made, he purchased me gifts. It was Christmas Eve and I was so excited because I knew I would get to see Billy and I thought he might have a gift for me. When we met for our regular date on Christmas Eve, he came with a gift just as I knew he would. Before he gave me the gift, he said, "I hope you like what I have for you. It is something I have heard you talk about many times. I opened the gift and the excitement and joy I felt overwhelmed me and I cried. It was the most beautiful, yellow Zenith clock radio. I hugged him and said to him, "I can now listen to my favorite radio programs on my own radio". "This is the best gift I have ever received".

I now had my own radio and I could listen to my favorite radio program "Our Best to You". This was a program that played love songs and I could listen to them and fall asleep thinking of Billy. Billy enjoyed giving me things when he could afford them.

There were many other nice gifts but one in particular was the biggest surprise. I had been at the movies on a Saturday afternoon and had just returned to the campus. As I entered my building, I noticed several excited girls standing outside my room. I asked them; "what is going on?" They replied: "Your roommate has just received a beautiful cedar hope chest as a graduation gift. I went inside our room and there it was a beautiful mahogany chest. I was happy for her but a little envious at the same time. Hearing all the noise and chatter, the matron in the building came up the steps and stopped at our room. She said; "Peggy, have you seen your graduation gift from Billy?" I said to her; "No, where is it?" "It is right there in your room, a cedar chest". I screamed; "you mean that chest is for me?" I proceeded to open it and it smelled so good inside. I could just imagine what it would be like to put all my special things in that chest.

I cherish that cedar chest then and I do now. I will pass it on to my daughter Brenda and she will pass it on, I am sure, to Stacey, her daughter.

* * *

Every student looked forward to graduating from the Methodist Orphanage High School, but it was a sad time as well. After living in the orphanage for twelve years it was hard to leave the safety and security of the only home we had ever known. It was scary as well as exciting. In later years I wrote a poem expressing my joy and concern when I had to leave the only home I had ever known.

THERE IS A PLACE

There is a place where memories dwell among the tall oak trees
With echoes of a squeaking swing, the mournful sound of a ringing bell. Do not weep
for those of us who knew this place so well
For we have secrets you do not know and secrets we must tell.

Are those our mothers I hear crying in the distance far away?
Do they weep for what might have been or what they had to do?
Do not weep, mothers, for yours was not by choice.
You saved a child and gave it a chance that day in July

Burwell Building

When you waved for the last time good-bye.

Is she as kind as her face seems? She is all in white so crisp and clean.
Would she take care of me today and what of tomorrow and the next day?
This building is big, of brick and stone, with windows beckoning for me to come.
There are many children, boys and girls playing in a room so large.
Who are these children looking at me? Will they be my friends and will they like me?
Night is dark and the bed is small. It seems so fresh and clean.
I hear footsteps in the hall. Be quiet and go to sleep. She is not my mother.
I feel no warmth but something tells me it will be okay.
My legs are short to walk so far. Breakfast is waiting and we must go
Like following the leader up the road.
There are little chairs at little tables with food so good to us. Before we eat we
Bow our heads while Daddy Barnes says grace.
I am not alone in this secret place for there are many tables everywhere.
There are big children and really big children.
Maybe I will see my big brothers or sister somewhere.

When I think of how it used to be together, my family and me, I want to cry but I dare not.
Have I forgotten my mother so fast? I seem to belong to this new place
I try to think of where she is and I feel sad again. Life is different and I learn the rules.
Do not wet your bed or lose your shoes.
Her face is sweet and full of love, this teacher I go to see.
It is my first day and I am ready to learn with my classmates and Miss Mary Ferree.
Her love of music and playing sticks makes it all fun after ABCs.
As I grow older my days are filled with ironing clothes, cooking, and serving food.
My brothers work on the dairy farm with other boys who are big and strong.
The chapel is a meeting place where we all go to hear
The Holy Message and what will happen if we sin and do not fear.
Their heads are bowed as they lean on the chairs in front of them.
Muh Brown watches closely to see that every head is down.
Sarah recites the beatitudes and I am so impressed.
I am not so good at performing. I think I will leave that to the rest.

An Exceptional Journey

It is summer and the swimming pool invites us all to play.
There is watermelon so red and juicy for all of us to share this day.
My mother visits and looks so proud. She thinks I am smart and I just laugh.
She seems so old with her wrinkled face, but I am happy in my new place.
I have been here longer than with her.
My life is filled with school, basketball, cheerleading and boyfriends.
What more could I want than this?
Is this the day I must leave this place? So many years have passed.
There are so many times to remember.
Will I ever be the same when all of this is gone?
What will I do? Where will I go when I leave this place with my Bible and trunk?
It is not so bad to sleep somewhere away from the buildings I have known.
I will go to college and become a secretary. Where will Frank and Robert go?
Will John and James stay close by? Will Billy wait for me?
There is a draft. Will they be called? And what about Mildred, Barbara, and Betty?
I bet Natalie will go to the coast and Colleen will play the piano somewhere.
Is this goodbye forever and ever? Will we meet again some day? Of course we will meet again.
You do not leave your brothers and sisters. We will meet year after year as
Doctors, lawyers, preachers, artists, and teachers.
We will hug and kiss and laugh a lot.
We will be together. How happy I am.

There is a place for memories inside each of us.
We know the work we are meant to do.
To the little children with sad eyes who cry out "please help us"
We will open wide our arms and hold them close
While we tell them secrets only we can tell
About a place where life goes on to the ringing of the bell.

* * *

Our graduation ceremony was not unlike a public school's. We had class night and junior and senior banquets. We wore beautiful, long, formal gowns for class night and the juniors entertained the senior class.

When graduation night came, we put on our caps and gowns to walk down the aisle at Memorial Auditorium, where all Raleigh high school students were given their diplomas together. The orphanage students wore caps and gowns that were just a little bit different in color from the others. This set us apart, but our names were listed in the program alphabetically with all of the other students. What a proud and wonderful occasion.

At one of the celebrations we were given Bibles to take out into the world with us. We were also given trunks to store our belongings. Some students would take these gifts to college; some of the boys would be drafted into military service; and some students would just go back to whatever relatives they had.

After graduation one of the orphanage girls named Barbara Ann and I rented a room a short distance from the orphanage, from two elderly sisters living together in a house. We shared the room but our rent did not include food or laundry. We could walk to a nearby drugstore and get sandwiches and milkshakes, and we lived off of this diet for the first few days.

Barbara Ann was enrolled in a local business college, and I started to look for a job. I had no skills but I had a lot of spunk and felt I could do anything. My first job was in a small shop selling hosiery and hats; I did better with the former than the latter. I can't remember how much money I made but it kept me in ham sandwiches and milkshakes.

I missed Billy but was able to see him often and it was nice to be together for the first time as adults. We could go to movies and drive around in a car. I also missed my orphanage brothers and sisters. I would lie in bed at night and wonder what they were doing and if I would ever see them again. Some of them went to faraway places; some of them even went overseas. It was difficult adjusting to my new life but thanks to my religious upbringing I was able to rely on my faith when fear and sadness overwhelmed me. I also relied on Billy. More and more he became my whole world and with him I could actually see a bright future. With him and what I had learned at the orphanage I could face whatever adversities I would encounter.

For both Billy and me, spending years with people who were just like us, with the same feelings about being in an orphanage, was a blessing. We made lifelong connections and learned many lessons that carried us through life.

The orphanage was a safe haven for many children who otherwise would have had nowhere to go. Sadly, it no longer exists. The buildings are gone; the big bell on top of the laundry will not ring to call children to breakfast, lunch, or supper. The swimming pool is gone and the infirmary is no longer there, but at our reunion on Easter Sunday when former students walk through Fred Fletcher Park, they can hear the laughter of the children playing in the park. It brings back memories for them when they were raised in the Methodist Orphanage and played on the green hills where now the park is located. They love their home and even though it no longer exists, they come back for an annual reunion every Easter to relive those years so long ago when they ran barefoot through the grass on the rolling hills of their home—the Methodist Orphanage.

Page Building

Billy

It was my first day at the orphanage and like so many before me I had to spend a few days in the infirmary, getting shots and being checked for any diseases that could be spread to the other children. The two nurses were so kind to my brother and me and made us feel welcome in our new home. Everyone loved the nurses because they understood how difficult it was to experience such a drastic change.

I was very inquisitive about my new surroundings. I looked out the infirmary window to a playground with large swings. A number of young girls were swinging and playing in the bright September sunshine. One of those girls would be very special to me in the future. Of course I didn't know it at the time but would be reminded of this first encounter years later.

After three days in the infirmary, my brother and I were assigned to the buildings we would live in for the next few years. I went to the Page Building and Donald was sent to the Borden Building. The Page Building was large, three stories, with wide front steps and many windows. I was impressed by it. At least thirty-five boys lived there with a matron. It had a large basement where we spent most of our time; the showers were there too as well as the compartments where we kept our meager belongings.

The second floor had rooms where we had supervised study hall and the matron's quarters. We slept on the third floor, with eight boys in some rooms and four boys in others. We were all about the same age—twelve and thirteen and in the seventh and eighth grades.

I had my very first Christmas at the orphanage while living in the Page Building. Before Christmas each child could make a wish for something as long as it didn't cost over two dollars. A Sunday school class at Edenton Street Methodist Church provided the gifts and brought them to the orphanage. We were treated to a massive tree in the auditorium and Santa Claus would call each child's name to come and receive their gift on Christmas morning.

My wish that year was for a box of Almond Joy candy bars. I was both surprised and amazed when my name was called and I did indeed receive a whole box of them. I had never had so much candy in my entire life, and I was very happy. The Woodmen of the World organization donated a big bag of fruit and nuts as well.

The other boys and I were all glad to show each other our gifts. When I showed one of the boys my candy bars, he offered me a really good deal. He said if I would give him an Almond Joy he would share some fruit his mother would bring him next time she visited. I thought that was a good offer and I gave him a candy bar.

Several months later I asked the boy about the fruit and he said to me, "What do you mean? Why do you think I'm in an orphanage? I don't have a mother." This was my first lesson in sharing and not expecting anything in return.

* * *

After being in the orphanage for a few weeks, I received my first letter from my grandmother. When I opened it I was shocked and happy to see a dollar bill. In the building where I lived there was a bully, so I thought I would use this money to get on his good side. I asked him to

Page Building

go to the Milky Way, a local store, to get some ice cream with me. Of course he accepted my invitation, and we went to get our treats.

I bought ice cream cones for both of us. We also shared an oatmeal cookie. I had eighty-five cents left. I took it back to the building and put it in my Bible because I thought even the worst person wouldn't violate the sacred book. I was wrong. When I opened my Bible the next day to share my fortune with another friend, the money was gone. I knew in my heart the bully had taken it because he was the only person who knew where it was. This was another lesson: be trusting, but not stupid.

* * *

Boys young and old at the orphanage seemed to have an interest in what the new boys were like and what kind of athletic skills they possessed. A number of them challenged me to throw a rock over a house in back of the Page building. I was keenly aware of the consequences if I hit one of the house's windows, so I threw the rock to make it fall just short. My performance must have been acceptable because from then on the boys included me in their activities every day.

I was a little older than most boys who entered the orphanage, so I was eligible to work on the orphanage's 280-acre farm. We raised hogs and grew hay and corn for our twenty-plus milk cows. One of my first assignments on the farm consisted of working in the silo, packing down the ground-up corn we fed the cows. Ten of us did this job continuously for several hours. We packed the corn until all of it had been ground and blown into the silo. It was hard and tedious work.

After several years of working on the farm, I was assigned to work in the school principal's office doing typing and filing and delivering papers to teachers. I liked this job because the principal took a special interest in me and taught me as much as he could about office work. It was much easier than stomping corn in a silo.

My next assignment, when I was fifteen years old, was working on the orphanage dairy farm. The dairy boys got up at 3:30 every morning and got on a rickety, open-end truck to make the trip to the farm. I worked in the milk house, where I made sure all the ten-gallon milk cans were full after they were sent through a filtering process. Most of the milk went to the children at the orphanage, but we did sell some to a local creamery. We would deliver it there, then head to the orphanage's kitchen with the rest, where we got a good, nourishing breakfast. Then we went back to our building to get some sleep.

My last assignment before graduating from the Methodist Orphanage High School was keeping the boiler running at the infirmary. We had coal heat, and the furnaces had to run constantly in the wintertime.

We enjoyed all three daily meals in a large dining room with girls seated on one side and boys on the other. We had good meals; my very favorite was a bowl of peanut butter, a jar of molasses, a pitcher of cold milk from our dairy, and a loaf of bread. We had this every Tuesday, Thursday, and Saturday. We called it "peanut butter and zip."

Six people sat around each table and we would share the food. We had a very special way of making the peanut butter and molasses go a long way: Each of us would put a pile of peanut butter in the middle of our plate and then pour the strong molasses over it. We would then stir it until it was well mixed and put bite-size portions of it onto our bread. You could get quite a few bites this way.

* * *

Boys will be boys, and we had a few tricks we enjoyed playing on the local folks when there were no matrons to stop us. One made us all laugh with joy when it worked perfectly. We would take an old tire and wrap it in white paper until it looked like a new tire. We would then go to one of the main streets in back of the orphanage and lay it right next to the curb, where it could easily be seen. Then we hid in the bushes. Cars would come by on a regular basis and for sure one driver would see the tire and slam on the brakes. But by the time he got back to look at it, we had already jumped out and take it into the woods with us. The driver would look all around, confused and disappointed. I don't remember any of us ever getting caught.

Page Building

One of the most influential people in my life at the orphanage was the matron of the Page Building. His name was Sam and he was like a father to us boys. He was young and single, and he had just completed his service to our country. He was athletic, and he enjoyed coaching and teaching young boys.

Sam taught us the fundamentals of baseball, football, and basketball. He coached the junior varsity football team and looked for his boys in the Page Building to participate in this sport. When the City of Raleigh sponsored track events, he took a few of the boys to see the competition. He got me interested in sports.

Soon after coming to work at the orphanage Sam met a beautiful lady who had also just arrived on campus to work. He told the superintendent he would marry that girl one day. He was determined to make her his. He later married Anna, and the boys in the Page Building had not only a father figure but also a new mom. He and Anna loved the boys and enjoyed teaching them and making sure they grew into fine young men, and they remained loyal to their boys long after they graduated from high school. The boys have stayed in touch as well. Sam passed away in 2001, and his boys were pallbearers at his funeral. They continue to visit and call Anna regularly.

At the orphanage, the other boys and I sometimes tried to get away with breaking the rules, but Sam was diligent in his observation of our coming and going. On one occasion several of us boys decided to sneak out and attend a professional baseball game off campus. Before leaving we fixed our beds to appear as though we were sleeping. After the game we attempted to sneak back into the building without being caught. We had just turned the corner to go up the stairs when I felt a hand on my shoulder. It was Sam—he had caught us. He gave us a serious lecture on what it meant to disobey, and just seeing the disappointment in his face was enough for us never to do it again.

We also made up games like fan out, where we would swing a stick like a bat at a tennis ball. Marbles were very popular, particularly with the boys. Some boys even won the city competitions. We played most every day and sometimes several times a day. Shooting marbles was always an exciting activity.

Sports helped us learn to play together as a team and get proper exercise. Being outdoors gave us the space to experiment and run about for hours on end. Our high school had football, basketball, baseball, and girl's softball teams and we were in the Class A District II conference with six other high schools: Chapel Hill, Durham County, Oxford, Oxford Orphanage, Henderson, and Roxboro.

Though 300 children lived at the orphanage and attended its private school, the ninth through twelfth grades had only eighty-two students. Of this number thirty-one were boys. In my senior year twenty-three of us participated in football. Although we were small in number and size, we had an extreme desire to win in all of the sports we played.

Our football season began in September with our coach waking us up each morning at 6:00. We met in front of the building we lived in and began our workout: jumping jacks, duck walking, pushups, and other strength-building activities. On some mornings we had to run what we called "around the block." The route was over one mile long and took us to one of the main streets in the city and through a very populated neighborhood. Anyone who didn't finish in time suffered the consequences, which meant running laps around the practice field. Sometimes the coach would drive his car to make sure we were running instead of walking. If he caught someone walking he had to do double laps.

After our morning exercises and breakfast, we would do the chores assigned to us, then go to school in the afternoon. Afterward we went straight to practice whatever sport was in season at the time.

Most of the staff at the Methodist Orphanage were encouraging. Sometimes, however, they were not. This could make a boy weak, or it could make him stronger. On one occasion a group of us were walking to breakfast with our coach and his wife. I remember how much I was looking forward to the football season, and I said with a lot of enthusiasm that I was going to be named to the all-conference football team at the end of the year.

The coach's wife heard me and responded, "You're too small even to be considered for that honor."

I agreed I was too small—I weighed only 130 pounds. But I was the starting right guard on offense and was the linebacker on defense. Our record for the year was six wins and four losses. At the end of the season I was named an honorary member of the all-conference team. While I didn't receive the highest honor, I felt I had reached my goal of being one of the best in the conference—and I had proven the coach's wife wrong.

Beginning in 1948 the Sudan Temple sponsored an annual Orphanage Bowl football game. That first year the Oxford Orphanage from Oxford and the Methodist Orphanage were chosen to participate. Each year a large parade announced the Orphanage Shrine Bowl game, which was played at the Riddick Stadium, North Carolina State College's home field. The game attracted hundreds of local fans and raised thousands of dollars for each orphanage's athletic program.

At the end of each football season, we had a banquet. Each of the players received a gold football pendant donated by the Sudan Temple. We wore the footballs proudly on chains attached to our belt loops. During one of our final banquets we had a special guest speaker: Wallace Wade, an outstanding Duke University football coach. We felt so special to have such a distinguished coach and we felt even more special when he congratulated each of us on a job well done.

* * *

Several months after I came to live at the orphanage, I received a letter from my mother. She had taken a job as a housemother at the Oxford Orphanage, which was supported by the Masons. My sister lived with my mother while she worked there and I got to see her once in a while, as our football, basketball, and baseball teams played against Oxford Orphanage and from time to time we traveled there to play.

Two years later my mother was offered a similar job at The Children's Home, an orphanage in Winston-Salem, serving the western part of

North Carolina and supported by the Methodist Church. The Methodist Orphanage served eastern North Carolina. My sister continued to live with my mother and graduated from Reynolds High School in 1950.

During my senior year my mother came to work at the Methodist Orphanage as the dining-room matron. She lived in an apartment in one of the girl's buildings, and my sister was allowed to live with her. While there my sister met an orphanage boy and they later married.

After working at the Methodist Orphanage my mother accepted a position with the Morehead School for the Blind in Raleigh. She worked there for several years. She was eventually diagnosed with a brain tumor and died at the age of fifty-six.

After spending two years in the Page Building I was assigned to the Cole Building. I was fourteen years old. The matron in this building was a math teacher at our high school. J. W. Bryan was a kind, funny man and was popular with all of the boys both in the building and in school. He never married but never seemed lonely because he had so many friends.

I remember how he used to sit in a chair and put one leg behind his head. All of us kids thought that was the funniest thing we had ever seen a grown-up do. He was a good teacher who made learning fun, and we all loved being in his class.

At the age of sixteen I moved to the Garris Building, where only the older boys lived. I was a junior in high school and had been living at the orphanage for five years. I had grown to love my home and all of my orphanage brothers and sisters. Life before the orphanage was a distant memory.

SUMMER AT THE ORPHANAGE

Peggy

Summer was always a special time when we were children. We loved our orphanage home and all those who played such major roles in our lives. We love to tell the stories, and there are many. All the memories are precious, and we cherish them.

We started looking forward to the fun as soon as school was over and the weather turned warm. We had jobs to do but we still had time to play, and with more than 300 playmates we could always find interesting things to do. Our favorite activity was swimming at the pool, where we could dive to our heart's content. Boys and girls could be in the pool together when we got older. When we were very young we swam in the baby pool and the big girls and boys or the matrons watched us very closely. .

Every summer we had a big watermelon cutting and we could eat all the red, juicy fruit we wanted until we were full. When it came time for the cutting, all 300 of us ran to the skating rink adjacent to the swimming pool, where the matrons had already cut the melons with the help of some of the older boys. Each of us was allowed to pick up a big slice of the melon and even a second piece as long as it lasted. There was, of course, a good watermelon rind fight after each of these get-togethers.

Most every child got his or her face rubbed with a melon rind before the activity was over.

The skating rink was constructed in 1920 and was a gift from the Raleigh Lions Club. Roller-skating was a very popular activity in the summertime and most of the children had skates or could borrow them from someone who did. They could be adjusted to fit any size and then tightened with a key. We would go around and around the rink believing we were the best skaters in the whole wide world.

Each year it seemed like summer would never end. We took advantage of every minute we had to enjoy the season. It was glorious to run barefoot through the grass on the rolling hills. It was a happy time to spend with so many brothers and sisters. After supper we could play for at least two hours before having to come in and get ready for bed. Oh, we got stone bruises and skinned knees, but injuries were rare and there was always the infirmary, where we could go and get patched up.

One thing is for certain: when we played, we played hard and when we worked, we worked hard. There was ironing to be done and meals to be served. There was also a big dairy farm with lots of cows to milk. There were floors to be waxed and leaves to be raked. Picking up sticks was the least favorite amongst the younger girls. Working in the kitchen was the least favorite of the older girls.

When we tell our story people are surprised to learn we took summer vacations while living at the orphanage. They always ask, "Where did you go if you didn't have people who could care for you?" In the summer months we were allowed to visit relatives if they were good and decent people—and if they had a place we could visit. Many parents worked and were not in positions to take their children for two weeks, but my siblings and I went home every summer. Our place to go may have been a tenant farmhouse with an outhouse and no running water, but it was a place.

My brothers left the orphanage before they finished school, so my memories of them going to see our mother are vague. However I vividly remember my younger sister and I visiting for the two weeks in the summer. We would go by bus to Louisburg, North Carolina, or wherever our mom could find a farmer who would let her share the crop for her efforts in the fields. Someone would meet us at the bus station and drive us to the country. We never knew whether we would be going to the same tenant farmhouse or another one, but they all looked very similar. They were generally unpainted clapboard, and this was the '40s so there was very little electricity and running water in rural North Carolina. We usually had none. Only the big, white house on the hill had those things because that was where the land owners lived.

There was never any grass in front of our house, but Mom swept the yard with a stick broom and made it look neat anyway. And there were almost always chickens and other farm animals wandering around. I remember one summer there were morning glories running up the side of the front porch. I was so pleased there were flowers at our house. I didn't know they were a wild vine that just grew in some places.

We loved staying with my mother and enjoyed the wide-open fields, where we could run and play all day. My older sister did most of the cooking while my mother handed tobacco in the tobacco fields. She would get up early and make huge pans of biscuits with eggs, fatback, and sometimes even fried chicken. We loved it because we didn't get that kind of food in the orphanage. We would have lots of vegetables and always lots of homemade biscuits. My mother made the best biscuits in the world, cooked on a wood-fired stove. It's a mystery to me how she knew when the stove was hot enough to cook the biscuits, but they were perfect. She had a little ash tray shaped like a miniature frying pan and she let my little sister and I cook a biscuit in that. It was so neat because we had our own little biscuit to share.

On many days we went to visit people who lived in the area, usually before dinnertime, and they always asked us to stay. I guess Mom needed to get food any way she could for her large family. But I knew at an early age this was a form of begging and I didn't like it.

Sometimes we would visit relatives. Two of my uncles had at least ten children each and we enjoyed visiting them and playing games together. They were just as poor as Mom but they at least had a mother and a father to take care of the children. Sometimes we had supper with them. It was better than going to a neighbor's.

It was quite a transition from the orphanage to a tenant farmhouse in the country. My sister and I were very young when we were taken to the orphanage so we had very few memories of living in the country. At the orphanage we had all of the modern conveniences. When we visited our mom in the country it was quite different. We slept on blankets on the floor and we bathed in a washtub outside. We went to the outhouse when we needed to and we drank water from a well. We rather enjoyed the differences, except when our brothers teased us as we attempted to bathe in private. It was also somewhat scary when we returned from the country store at night to a dark house, and our mom would have to go in first to light the kerosene lamps. I thought she was the bravest person I ever knew. She didn't seem to be afraid of anything.

Going to the country store was often the evening's entertainment. Most of the time we rode there in the back of a wagon pulled by a mule. When we got to the store the old folks would sit around and talk. The children would play hide-and-seek or other games. When we were visiting from the orphanage our mother just loved to make my sister and me sing for the older folks. We didn't like it, but we did it any way. She was so proud of us.

I remember one time when my mother took some chicken-feed sackcloth and made my sister and me the cutest little shorts outfits out of it. The material was printed with little flowers and was really pretty. She also bought us some sandals that summer and pretty headbands. We were so proud of those outfits and wore them when we returned to the orphanage.

As we got a little older, when we visited our mother we would spend time with her at the barn. She let me hand tobacco one time and I made seven dollars for the week. It was the most money I'd ever had. I took it back to the orphanage and gave it to the matron to keep for me. Then my older brother, who had a drinking problem, came to see me. He told me my mother was on the outskirts of town and needed the money to get a tire fixed so she could come see me. He took my seven dollars, and when he left I realized mother was not coming. Years later, when I was a teenager, he felt bad about doing this to me and bought me a bathing suit, which was important to me at the time. He later died in a car accident after a drinking binge.

In my late teen years, visiting my mother was not a pleasant experience. My older brothers were grown and had gotten married. My older sister had also gotten married and moved away. Mom had moved to the town of Henderson, in an area called Moccasin Bottom and Flint Hill, where most of the people who worked in the cotton mills lived. The area had nothing positive about it, but the people who worked in the mills were good and hard working and tried their best to make lives for their families. Their houses were very similar in design and very small. There were no paved streets, and during the night I could hear fights outside.

On one occasion my brother and brother-in-law got into a vicious fight over something stupid. My mother chose to side with her son and injected herself into the fight. It was one of the scariest times of my life and I will never forget it. I loved my brother and didn't want him to be hurt, and I certainly didn't want my mother hurt. It was soon obvious my mother would take care of herself, and the fight ended without too much harm done to anyone.

I didn't like being there and I don't think the orphanage would have allowed me to go if they knew the circumstances. I knew what it meant to be poor but I didn't understand why some people had to live in certain conditions while others lived in luxury. I knew I didn't want to end up like the mill people. I wanted to make something of myself and provide a good and happy life for my family.

I think it was a hardship for my mom to have me for a whole week or two. She didn't have the money to feed me, and she certainly couldn't pay for me to enjoy any entertainment. By this time my sister had also left the orphanage leaving just me to finish my schooling. I was dating Billy and he came to get me when my two week vacation was over. He did not like what he saw and told me I would not be going back.

I was heartbroken when my sister, Ann, left the orphanage at the age of fourteen. My mother took her out and it was the worst mistake she ever made. She did it hoping to get more money in her welfare check.

When my sister told the social services lady she hadn't asked to go home and she wanted to stay in the orphanage, the lady told our mother she wouldn't get more money. This made it very difficult for Ann. Our mother resented having to feed her and certainly could not give her money for lunch at school. Ann had no money for new clothes either and soon just quit school. She got married that same year and her life was not easy from that time on. She was much too young to be married and soon she was pregnant. She gave birth to her first child at the age of fifteen years.

The baby had a heart defect and didn't live but a few months. Ann was devastated when she lost her baby but it was not long before she was pregnant again. She gave birth to a beautiful little girl and she was so happy. Ann was a good mother; she took very good care of her daughter. She and her husband struggled financially, but his mother and father helped out, so they got by. Ann had three more children—all boys. We stayed in touch with each other but our lives took different directions. She was always special to me and I always thought she was the most beautiful little sister any one could have. We are close today and see each other often.

* * *

Billy

Some of the orphanage kids had summer vacations that were different from mine. They couldn't go home for one reason or another and instead spent time with kind and generous families who took several children to stay with them. I was one of the children who needed a place to go because his mother was working. I remember the summers vividly. I recall:

During my first summer at the orphanage, my brother, Donald, and I were told we would be enjoying our vacation at a camp in Hendersonville, North Carolina, sponsored by the Elks Club of the Carolinas. We took a bus there and enjoyed a fun-filled two weeks with lots of other boys. We did the regular camp activities including swimming, canoeing, baseball and, singing around the campfire. We slept on bunk beds and ate in a big dining hall. The camp counselor was the son of a prominent politician; the son became very well known when he opened a steakhouse which still stands today and is one of the finest restaurants in North Carolina.

My brother and I were able to spend time with our grandmother and younger brother during our second year at the orphanage. Our grandmother lived in the country, in a little town called Cash Corner. It was next to Vandemere in Pamlico County. This was a fishing community where many boats left early in the morning to get the first catches.

I learned to eat raw oysters that summer and still love them to this day. My grandfather took me to the backyard, where he had a bucket of raw oysters and a bowl of vinegar. He proceeded to open an oyster with a knife and then dip it in the vinegar and eat it. He repeated this process but handed me the oyster. I ate it and while the taste did not appeal to me at first, it grew on me, and we enjoyed eating oysters for at least an hour before we got our fill.

I liked going to my grandparent's home. They owned their land and the house, a two-story structure with two bedrooms upstairs and one master bedroom downstairs. There was no running water or electricity but I thought the house was perfect. It had a big front porch with a swing, and it was screened in so we could sit out and not worry about the bugs. The one thing I didn't like about the house was how cold it was in the wintertime. The only source of heat was a wood stove downstairs in the living room. My grandmother would light it every morning before we got up. At night we would pile as many blankets as we could find on top of us to keep warm.

In my third year at the orphanage, I volunteered to stay for the summer to do work around the campus and on the farm. Because few children were left during summer vacation, we ate in a special dining room. For one meal we were served rutabagas, a white vegetable that has the most awful taste to me. I tried to eat them because I was expected to, but I promised myself that day I would never again eat a rutabaga as long as I lived. I have kept my promise—I have not eaten a rutabaga since.

My brother and I were happy the next year when we received an invitation from our aunt to visit her in Gates, a small town in northeastern

North Carolina. My aunt and uncle lived across the street from a peach orchard and they told us we could eat all the peaches we wanted. We did, and we got so tired of them, by the time we left we were not interested in peaches anymore.

My last summer at the orphanage was a little different in that we went to stay with a perfect stranger. She was a very nice lady who took us in along with three other orphanage children—two sisters and their brother. This lady's son delivered concrete blocks to construction sites and I would go along with him to help him load and unload the blocks.

One of the best vacations we ever experienced was when the senior class had the opportunity to go to Manteo, North Carolina, a coastal town where an outdoor drama called *The Lost Colony* was performed. In addition to enjoying the play we visited Kill Devil Hill, where the Wright Brothers took their first airplane flight. We also had plenty of time to spend on the beach and swim in the ocean. Many of us had never seen the ocean. We went on a bus and enjoyed singing and playing games while we traveled to the coast.

I was glad when summer vacation was over because I missed my orphanage brothers and sisters, and I particularly missed seeing Peggy. . However, I knew one day we would spend every summer vacation together, and that was what kept me going through the years.

My Special Angel

Peggy

School at the orphanage was pretty much the same as public school, and I did reasonably well but not great. I had no intentions of going to a college or university. Most of the girls who graduated from the Methodist Orphanage High School would go on to business school or study nursing.

When I was fourteen years old, an amazing thing happened. I loved to sing, and the music teacher thought I could benefit from piano lessons. They weren't free; there was a small charge and if a family member or some benefactor could help, any student could take lessons. Mr. B.G. Thompson, a generous and kind man from Goldsboro, North Carolina, agreed to finance my lessons. I remember they were seven dollars per month.

Even though I wasn't musically gifted, I enjoyed the lessons. I even enjoyed dressing up in a long gown and performing at the recitals held in the big auditorium, with all of the students watching and listening. On one occasion I was scheduled to play a duet with Billy's very talented brother. The piece was "March Military" and I played the bass part. I forgot my place while playing and whispered to Donald, "I need to start over."

He said to me, "Just begin where you lost your place."

I said I couldn't and started to play the beginning of the piece. I was so embarrassed and felt awful for Donald because he was so respected as a musician and I had made us both look like fools. He took it well and still won an award that year for his musical talents.

The fact that Mr. Thompson would do something so nice for me even though he didn't know me at all made me feel special. I met him later on and enjoyed getting to know him. He was ninety-one years old and practically deaf. When he talked to me he yelled so loud I thought he was mad. I had to write down everything I wanted to say to him and he would read my notes and smile.

On my first visit with him in Goldsboro, I took a friend with me. I was rather shy, and going away by myself to such a big mansion was frightening. Well, it got to be more frightening than I had counted on. During the night my friend and I had access to the kitchen and ate more than we should have. I think it was bananas. I got sick and vomited in the tub. The housekeeper came to help us and filled the tub with water.

I don't remember much more until the next morning at breakfast. To my horror water begin to drip from the ceiling. Mr. Thompson yelled out, "Overrunning bathtub!" I was scared to death because I didn't know how the bathtub had gotten so full of water. I didn't remember putting any water in it. Many years later we were told the housekeeper was responsible, but that didn't help my sense of guilt.

Mr. Thompson died before I graduated from high school. Daddy Barnes, the superintendent of the orphanage, called Mr. Thompson's three sons to see if they would like to continue paying for my lessons. One of them was named Bruce and he said he wasn't interested in sponsoring a girl but would entertain working with a young boy. However, he sent me a letter and enclosed a check for $25. I had money for the first time in my life. I purchased an Easter suit, a pair of gloves, and a hat. I wrote to Mr. Thompson, thanked him for the money, and told him what I had purchased. We continued to correspond on a weekly basis.

After that Mr. Thompson contacted the superintendent to see if he could be my sponsor for everything I would need while living at the orphanage. Daddy Barnes told me about the request and asked me what

I thought of it. I told him I already had a sponsor who had been there for me from the very beginning. He suggested we write to Mr. Thompson and ask him to support another child who did not have a sponsor. I did this and my unselfishness seemed to impress him—he agreed.

Just before my graduation from high school, Mr. Thompson called to see if I would like to take a business course at a university. I was very reluctant to go away from Billy for very long, but he encouraged me. So I planned to enroll in a one-year commercial course at Woman's College in Greensboro in the fall.

Mr. Thompson sent me a gift of $125 for a graduation present, and that was by far the most money I had ever seen. It was enough to rent a room off campus.

My eating habits must have caused my health to suffer because I fainted one day while visiting the drug store and was unable to go to work for a day or two. I was weak and anemic from my poor diet and the general changes that had taken place in my life. Mr. Thompson had stayed in touch with me and called to check on me after I fell ill. He asked me why I was working and I told him I needed the money to eat and pay my rent until school started.

He said, "You don't need to work. I'll take care of you until school starts. You need to rest and get ready for school." He told me he was going to visit me and we would talk more then.

Within two weeks, he drove up to the home where my roommate and I lived. I was surprised by his appearance. He was a small man with thinning hair and a sharp nose. He drove up in a Model T Ford. I knew nothing of wealth but I thought all rich people drove big cars like Cadillacs. He brought me a chocolate cake and took my roommate and me out for lunch. I was amazed by his thoughtfulness and it was good finally to meet the man who had made such a difference in my life.

Before leaving he spoke to me about college. He told me his sister-in-law would be paying me a visit to help me get the things I would need. He also told me I probably would not like her very much, but that she was smart and plenty capable of helping me. I guess this answered my question about how I would get what I needed to enter college.

Mr. Thompson's sister-in-law showed up one day to take me shopping for school. Mr. Thompson was correct when he'd said I would not like her. She was bossy and curt. She was not unkind but very businesslike. We went shopping and she left no stone unturned. She purchased me sweaters, skirts, sheets, pillowcases, lamps, bedspreads, curtains, and everything I possibly could have needed including a dictionary. I felt like the richest girl in the world.

September came soon and I was off to college to study business for one year. Upon arriving I found my dorm and met my roommate. How ironic that I would get the richest girl in the dorm and she would get an orphanage girl as a roommate. She was a very nice person and did not seem spoiled at all. We set up our room with curtains, bedspreads, lamps, and, of course, our boyfriend's pictures on the dresser. This dorm was called Kirkland Hall. Only commercial students lived there. It was going to be fun and not unlike living at the orphanage—except the room I'd had at the orphanage was much nicer.

I wasn't prepared for college, and it soon showed in my grades. The business course consisted of typing, shorthand, office machines, and bookkeeping. I had never typed and I had never seen or written a check, so I was behind the eight ball from the very beginning. I was not concerned. After all I was going to have fun, and that was important to me.

I started in a beginner's typing class and discovered I had a real talent for it. I was typing more than seventy-five words per minute within a few weeks and later reached a speed of more than one hundred words per minute. I got my first job when I interviewed for a position with an employment agency. After taking the typing test the owner asked if I would like to work for him. Of course I accepted his invitation and worked for him for five years on a part-time basis. I later worked for some architects and they thought I was a pretty good typist as well. I stayed with them for five years before moving on to my final job as a human resources professional.

When I was exposed to accounting while attending college, I found it more than challenging. I had no idea what I was doing when a practice set was placed in front of me and I was told to balance a set of books.

The professor was astounded that I was so unprepared and asked me after class which high school I had attended. She thought I had gone to the largest in Raleigh. I told her I hadn't, and she mentioned another one—the second largest. I told her I hadn't attended that one either. She then naturally thought I had attended a private school. I told her I'd gone to the Methodist Orphanage High School. She suddenly looked at me in a different light and helped me all she could. It was pretty hopeless, but I can't say she didn't try.

Mr. Thompson was so generous to me while I was attending college. He sent me $25 a week for spending money—enough to buy my best friend and me an occasional hotdog at the local stand. I was also able to help Billy pay for gas when he could visit me on campus.

Before the year was out Mr. Thompson was signing his letters to me as Uncle Bruce. That seemed appropriate since he was one of the best things that had ever happened to me in my entire life. I had never enjoyed such kindness from anyone but Billy, and I felt so special and blessed. I left Woman's College with good skills to help me get a job, and my relationship with Uncle Bruce was not over by a long shot.

While I was attending school Billy presented me with an engagement ring and asked me if I would marry him. Of course I said yes; I had been determined to marry him since I was fifteen years old. He picked the gymnasium at the orphanage to give me a ring. This was very appropriate since both he and I loved basketball and had played for four years while in high school.

I returned to Raleigh and found a room to rent in a big house on Hillsborough Street. I wasn't too happy there because I felt so alone for the first time in my life. There were several other girls living in the same house but I didn't know them and was too busy looking for a job to get to know them. I finally found work with a wholesale distributor of household appliances. I was hired to do secretarial work for the accounting manager. The CEO of the company just happened to be on the board of directors of the Methodist Orphanage. My having lived there scored a few points for me. He reminded me during the interview that my fiancé worked for another wholesale distributor—a competitor. I didn't even know what "business competition" meant but I told him

An Exceptional Journey

I would not tell Billy anything about the company. I believe he knew I was not a serious risk to his business. It would be many years before I was even knowledgeable enough to even discuss business.

Billy and I planned to marry as soon as he paid off his car and we could save a little money. We were still corresponding with Mr. Thompson and he liked it when Billy and I would visit him in his home. One day he asked us when we planned to get married. We told him of our plans and he said to us, "You don't need to pay for two places to live when you plan to marry. Why don't you get married now and save money on rent?" He told us he would give us $500 to get us started.

We got to work on our plans. My wedding dress was the first thing to buy. I picked out a beautiful cocktail-length, lace dress and put it on layaway. Next we picked the Joseph G. Brown Chapel at Edenton Street Methodist Church to have our wedding. This is one of the oldest and largest Methodist churches in Raleigh, and it was where the orphanage students attended church and Sunday school. Next we had to find a preacher who would agree to marry us. The superintendent of the orphanage in 1954 was Reverend Forrest Hedden. He had taken me and my siblings to the orphanage in 1941. What a coincidence that Billy and I should have this kind man to marry us after so many years. He agreed to perform the ceremony and we picked August 28, 1954 for the blessed event.

It was such an exciting time for us. We knew our lifetime dream of being together would finally become a reality. Uncle Bruce loved us and we knew he would do anything to make us happy. We discussed asking him give me away at our wedding. . We met with him and I asked him "Uncle Bruce, would you be kind enough to honor me by giving me away at our wedding?" He replied "I can't accept that honor because there are so many people who have played major roles in your life. They deserve to have that privilege and not me". I was disappointed but not surprised because he was such an unassuming man. He suggested Daddy Barnes take me down the aisle. After all he was the only father I had ever known. He had been the superintendent and the daddy to hundreds of children for more than thirty-three years. Uncle Bruce then said; "I will be happy to sign your marriage certificate as a witness". We were honored that he would play a major role on our special day.

We thought everything was set until Uncle Bruce asked us what time the reception would be. We responded that we did not plan to have one.

He said, "Of course you'll have a reception. Every bride and groom has a reception after the wedding."

We began to think of just how we would go about having a reception since neither one of us had ever attended one. Uncle Bruce told us not to worry, he would take care of everything, and he promptly called Reverend Hedden to make the plans. Our heads were spinning as things begin to happen all around us. Billy's brother, Donald, was an accomplished musician and would play the piano. The superintendent's daughter would sing. Everything was set.

The day arrived and we were ready. We had rented a little garage apartment in an older section of Raleigh and the car was paid for. We even had money left to go on a honeymoon in Williamsburg, Virginia. We felt so blessed and so happy we could hardly contain ourselves.

The wedding went off without a hitch. We had a professional photographer take pictures. After the reception, we got into our 1953 Plymouth and started our drive to Williamsburg and the Blue Ridge Mountains. We were so young and so innocent it was amazing we even got to our rented cabin. We went to a nice restaurant for dinner. The hostess stopped us before we were seated and told Billy he would have to put on a sport coat before we could enjoy dinner. We promptly left and went to a small hamburger place where our clothes were more appropriate.

We enjoyed knowing we had a lifetime together ahead of us, and it was going to be a joyful and happy life. At last we were together forever, and nothing could change that. We were a happy couple and looked forward to all the good things that would come our way in the future. We were too optimistic to think of anything that was not positive.

It was about a year into our life together when I discovered I was pregnant. We hadn't planned to have children so early but we felt it was God's plan and accepted the joyful news with mixed emotions. I was nineteen years old and Billy was twenty. I continued to work until I began to show significantly. Then we decided I should quit work and stay home to prepare for the baby. This meant Billy needed to make extra money, so he started delivering papers in the morning and also reconciled a set of books for an automotive company. Of course he still worked at his full-time job every weekday and one half day on Saturday.

At the same time we decided to look for a larger apartment. Uncle Bruce approached us with the offer of a gift: he would purchase a house for us in a subdivision in Raleigh. He told us to look for one and give him a call when we found one we liked.

We met with a Realtor and he showed us a really nice subdivision. The Realtor told us there were no houses currently under construction for us to look at, but he had a lot of plans for us to pick from. We picked one we liked and called Uncle Bruce to tell him of our progress. He was not happy that we hadn't found a house he could see. He told us we weren't mature enough to have a home at that time because we didn't know how to look for a house that was already built.

He was right. We didn't know how to go about looking for anything because we had never purchased anything larger than an automobile. He offered to buy us some furniture for an apartment and we went that route. We found a really nice apartment with two bedrooms. We moved in with new furniture and set up the nursery for our first child. It was so cute.

Our beautiful daughter, Brenda, was born on February 5, 1956. She was perfect in every way and we felt God had given us such a precious little darling of our very own. There was just one thing we didn't count on: we didn't have a clue how to raise a baby, and there were no family members to help. God answered our prayers for guidance and knowledge in caring for our newborn baby. Our instincts kicked in and we began a journey with our daughter that would bring us untold joy and happiness.

We continued to rely on God's help as we worked through various issues faced by all young and inexperienced parents. Billy worked so hard to support us, and I stayed at home and looked after our little girl. I think we did a really good job. She was a healthy and happy child and brought us more joy than we ever could have imagined.

My Special Angel

In the summer of 1957 I was asked if I could fill in at a local television station while the regular receptionist was on vacation. We had never left our daughter, and it was not something we wanted to do. We thought long and hard and decided if I could work for a couple of weeks we could save the money for Christmas, and that would help a lot. We put our daughter in a daycare and I went to work at the television station. I made a few hundred dollars and it was good to know we could have a nice Christmas.

However, the television station had some personnel issues with one of the promotion clerks and asked me if I could stay for a while longer. The lady was ill and was not expected to return to work. We decided I could work for a year or so, to save enough money to make a down payment on a new home. We hated leaving our daughter in daycare but felt she would be happy in a new home with our own yard. She would have a lot of playmates in the neighborhood.

After I worked for almost a year we had enough money for a down payment. It was so exciting to think we could own a home. Uncle Bruce was right: we hadn't been mature enough to have a house when he'd offered to help us, but we were now and we had worked for it ourselves.

While I was pregnant with our son, I continued to work. I worked until almost my due date and resigned to have the baby and be a stay-at-home mom once again. Bruce was born on November 26, 1959. He was a handful from the moment he was born but was a joy to us and Brenda. She loved her little brother and she helped me look after him. We were a family and best of all we had our own home. We were so proud of what we had accomplished.

Of course, we could never forget the wonderful support Uncle Bruce had given us. He moved to a hotel in Goldsboro after his stepmother passed away. Uncle Bruce made the decision to move into the hotel so he could receive his meals and be around people. I believe he was in his sixties at the time. I told him on one of our visits that if I gave birth to a son I would name him Bruce because he had been so kind to me and made me feel so special for the first time in my life.

While I was pregnant Uncle Bruce fell in his hotel room. He was taken to the hospital and when we went to visit him we told him how much we loved him. He died shortly after that visit. I learned so much about him after his death. I wasn't the only person he had helped over the many years he lived. He'd helped many people in need and left his estate to the poor and indigent in Goldsboro. When our son was born I was proud to name him William after his father and Bruce after Uncle Bruce. He knows the story and is proud to have the name today.

Mabel "Muh" Brown

Billy

As a little girl, Mabel Brown loved her middy blouses. She wore white in summer, light blue in spring, and navy-blue serge in the winter. She always thought those were just the prettiest things. She wanted winter to come because she liked the red ties.

The middy blouses in those early years were the girls' uniform at the Methodist Orphanage. Mabel was one of eighty-five orphans there, admitted at age eight in September 1906 with her sister, Josephine. Her father was dead; her mother was ill and died the following April. Mabel was a typical ward of the home.

"We were really orphans" she often said. The campus was in the country then, a little world unto itself with its own school, dairy farm, and vegetable plot. "We didn't know there was anything uptown but ribbons and candy."

When my sister and I came to the orphanage, we knew it was home for the both of us. In those days the children lived in dormitories or large cottages with about thirty of their fellow students. They ate in a central dining hall and went to school on campus. Mabel stayed at the home until she graduated from high school there in 1918. When she left the orphanage she took a job making ladies' hats in Raleigh. But a flu epidemic brought her back to the home. She then began working there, first as a supervisor of the dining hall and later as a cottage mother, in the soda shop and then in the office, collecting coupons, until she retired in 1981. She said upon retirement, "I cried when I went there and I cried when I left."

The Methodist Conference chartered the institution in 1898. The next year the Methodists received a charter from the state legislature for an orphanage with the help of the Raleigh Chamber of Commerce and the citizens of Raleigh, who donated $3,000. The Methodist Conference purchased a portion of a site on Glenwood Avenue. It was expanded to sixty-four acres in 1908. The home eventually consisted of twenty-three buildings and the administration, dining room, and infirmary. At first a main building served all the orphanage's functions. In 1911 and 1913 dormitories for the both boys and girls were built.

Muh was a laughing woman with a halo of white hair. One of her boys who lived in her cottage when he arrived at the orphanage at age eleven fondly remembers eating molasses and peanut butter for a Saturday night meal and using an old sock for a football. He also remembers Muh. He said, "If you had a word to describe her it would be 'love'."

Another one of her boys wrote to Muh: "Thanks for all the kindness and love I received from you while at the Methodist Orphanage. Thank you for asking for me to go to the Brown Building from the Baby Cottage so I wouldn't have to go to the Borden Building. It made a big change in my life."

After living on her own for a while, Muh moved to a rest home. She always peppered her conversation with stories about the boys, to expressions of gratitude from her friends and outbursts of delighted laughter. She always said, "I was good to them and I made them mine."

In April 1990, at the annual Easter Reunion of the Methodist Orphanage, alumna Muh was honored for her many years of loving service to young children and the home. Approximately 250 people were in attendance as a plaque was presented to her. Songs were sung, poems were recited, and stories were told about Muh's loving service and leadership at the home. After the presentation of the plaque, Muh recited a poem of her own and limericks she had learned as a child growing up at the orphanage just after the turn of the century.

The inscription on the plaque given to her read:

> We salute and thank Mabel "Muh" Brown
> For her years of caring dedication
> To the Methodist Home for Children and to the
> Many, many children whose lives
> Her loving kindness touched. She
> Continues today to be an inspiration and a
> Guiding light for all of us who will never fill
> But lovingly follow in her footsteps.

Our beloved Muh died at the age of ninety-seven. Muh never married or bore children. and did not know her family well. She spent most of her life living and working at the Methodist Orphanage. Muh made her own home and family, drawing people in with her laughter and love of life. She raised scores of boys at the orphanage, where she was tagged as "Muh" for her motherly ways.

"My little children made me that for a love name," she often said. The following is in memory of her.

IN MEMORIAM
MABEL "MUH" BROWN

> August 27, 1898–August 3, 1995
> It is with deep sadness that we acknowledge the recent death of
> Mabel "Muh" Brown
> An alumna and former employee of the Methodist Orphanage/
> Methodist Home for Children (MO/MHC),
> Muh was "mother" to hundreds of boys and girls during
> The years she served the Methodist Orphanage and Methodist Home for Children

We miss Muh tremendously but take solace in our memories of her warmth, love, spirit, and humor.

Her funeral was held at the Garner United Methodist Church to an overflowing crowd. I gave the eulogy:

> During our many talks and visits with our beloved Muh Brown, she often said to my wife Peggy and me, "When I die, I don't want it to be a solemn occasion." Muh didn't like solemn occasions. We all remember her wonderful sense of humor. She would say to us, "When I die, I don't want any male pallbearers, because if they didn't want to take me out when I was alive, I don't want them taking me out when I am gone." How we laughed and marveled at her zest for life, and we remember what she meant to all of us who lived at the Methodist Orphanage. She was the mother to hundreds of little boys who, by fate, were placed in her loving care. How blessed we were to have this special lady at a time in our lives when we needed understanding and love.

A little boy sat on the steps of the Brown Building and cried as if his heart would break. This was his first week at the Methodist Orphanage in Raleigh, North Carolina. He had been assigned to the Brown Building to live for at least two years. The nicest lady came out of the building and sat down on the steps beside him. She put her arms around his shoulders and said, "I know you are sad and you miss your home." She held him tighter as he sobbed and said to him, "I'll take care of you and see that nothing hurts you."

That nice, sweet lady was our dear Muh Brown. She had a most precious gift to be able to stop the tears when no one else could. She had the heart and soul of an angel as she opened her arms and her heart to every child who came to live at the Methodist Orphanage in Raleigh.

I believe God made only one like Muh, and many of you here today feel the same way. I know this because I have seen the love and affection you have for her. I have seen you give of yourself and laugh and cry with her. How blessed we are to have known this wonderful angel. How blessed we are that she touched our lives with so much love and unselfishness.

She knew what God's plan was for her, and she never questioned the direction He chose for her. Her life was surely blessed when she gave up everything to be with children who needed her and would be better and more secure because of her.

We only have one life to live, and live it she did. She never missed or wanted the material things in life. She only wanted to give love and strength to those less fortunate. She never missed having a family of her own because she had a family of her own in all the children she cared for and loved with all her heart. She never missed the big house, the big car, jewels, or money. These things were not important to her. She had the most treasured thing of all…she had her children with her until the end.

However this is not the end for Mabel "Muh" Brown. This is just the beginning for her in a kingdom where streets are made of gold and everything is peaceful and wonderful. Is this not what we want for her today? Sure we will miss her, but she will be waiting for each of us in that place where we all will meet again. She is not gone but with us always as we remember the sweet words she shared with us about when she first went to the orphanage herself and had to leave her mother. A prayer she and her sister said to her mother at night.

An Exceptional Journey

> Goodnight Mama
> Sweet as a rose
> How much we love you
> God only knows
> Goodnight Mama
> Sweet as a rose
> How much we'll
> Miss you
> God only knows
> Goodnight Muh Brown
> Sweet as a rose
> Rest in peace for your
> Children will be with
> You always

One of her boys, Karl, wrote "A Few Words About Muh" after her death.

Muh Brown spent her entire life of almost ninety-seven years giving to others and spreading love, hope, comfort, and encouragement to children who came to the orphanage, and she left this world with little more than she came into it with.

It was no misnomer that she was called Muh, for she was the mother many of the orphanage boys and girls did not have and was a more real mother than the real mothers many of us did have. When we cried in our loneliness, she hugged us and told us all would be well. When we felt hopeless, she gave us hope. When we were frightened, she made us feel safe. When we felt discarded and worthless, she made us feel valued and worthwhile. She was the anchor that kept us secure on the stormy sea of our dislocation.

Muh came from the same place all the rest of us came from (extreme poverty), and she grew up, just like we did, in the orphanage without a single varying element. Yet through the rest of us who were flawed and flogged by despair, anger, self-doubt, loneliness, self-loathing, self-absorption, jealousy, resentment, envy, and little dishonesties, Muh was everlastingly serene, gentle, uncritical, happy, and completely content with her life.

Though without much formal education, she had some kind of inspired, instinctive understanding of all modern psychology teaches about raising children and more. She had not much physical authority, tiny little person that she was, but those under her care minded her without question. She would catch us doing something right and tell us about it. And when we did wrong, she corrected us with kindly regret.

Everyone she touched, child or adult, she made better. One could not help but smile in her presence. Sometimes her door was closed for a long time and we knew she was sick. But she never complained.

She never owned a house, or a car, or fine jewelry, or fancy clothes; she never traveled more than a hundred miles from Raleigh. But she seemed somehow endowed with gifts that transcended earthly pleasures and possessions.

How could this be so, that she took so much happiness simply by making others happy? Could it be that she was sent to be an angel among us, that her appointed mission in life was to hold our hands and soothe us with loving smiles through our hard passage? No other explanation makes as much sense.

Other Thoughts About Muh Brown From Former Alumnae

*"Muh truly cared about us when we were children,
knowing that was when we needed someone the most."
—Charles*

*"Loving, caring, supportive, always a big smile, good sense of humor. Muh always remembered our names—her memory and recall were tremendous— and I think she probably cared about us more than anybody else. She was all the boys's favorite person."
—Paul*

An Exceptional Journey

"Muh was the dream parent every kid wants to have. She was peace, love, hugs, and all the good images of family. When talking about the children at the orphanage, she would say, "I make them mine, then I make them mind."
Although I didn't live in her building, Muh made me hers, and I made her mine.
I think she gave all of us the foundation for the feeling of family we now share as brothers and sisters of the orphanage.
As long as she was around, I knew I would get my share of hugs and love.
She became my example as I grew up.
I saw Muh three times a day, every day, in the dining room.
She'd ring the bell to get our attention and say,
"Y'all be quiet and we'll have the blessing."
Then she would circulate around the room with a big pitcher of milk, always cheerful but not excessively so—making sure we all had plenty of milk to drink. She'd speak to each of us, giving us the individual recognition we craved. Muh made our lives at the orphanage a little easier.
Her strong, cheerful presence was a good influence on my life."

—Al

Birthday Parties In New Hill

Peggy

We loved our home in New Hill, North Carolina. It was located on fifteen acres of woods. Some years after we moved in we had an acre pond constructed on the property. It was beautiful and we stocked it so the grandchildren could enjoy fishing.

The house was in a beautiful country setting and was perfect for outdoor entertaining. We wanted to honor some of the people who had been so instrumental in our upbringing at the orphanage. This gave us the perfect opportunity to have a pig picking and invite our orphanage brothers and sisters. One of the people we loved so much and wanted to entertain was Muh Brown. She was in her early nineties when we decided to surprise her with a birthday party. We sent out a few invitations to our orphanage brothers and sisters and scheduled the party. Muh was to be brought to our woods without knowing she was going to be celebrating her birthday with us. When she arrived and saw so many of her orphanage children there to greet her, she was all smiles.

The pig was cooking on the grill and snack food was on the table under the gazebo. Everyone settled in to enjoy the afternoon and to wish Muh a happy birthday. She opened her gifts and read the many cards telling her how much we all loved her and would never forget the kindness she had shown us while living at the orphanage. This first party started a tradition with approximately twenty-five alumni attending. The next birthday party grew in attendance to forty five. Approximately a hundred alumni attended the last birthday party we had for Muh. We celebrated her birthday for six years until she passed away at the age of ninety-seven. She loved her parties and looked forward with great anticipation for each birthday to come so she could come to New Hill and celebrate.

After Muh passed away we really missed having the pig pickings and birthday parties. We wanted to continue honoring and celebrating with someone who had meant a lot to so many of us. The one other person who had made such a difference in so many lives was Sam Hudson, a matron in the Page Building, where boys aged twelve and thirteen had lived. He had been a young, energetic man with a military background. He'd loved sports and introduced athletics to many young boys when they'd come to the orphanage to live. They'd loved it and respected Sam. He'd been a strict but fair disciplinarian. He loved the boys and they knew it.

Billy and I got to work planning a ninetieth birthday party for Sam. The theme would be Sam's boys, and we would serve barbecue and all of the fixings. Again we sent out invitations to our orphanage brothers and sisters. More than seventy-five people came to wish Sam a happy birthday. We had a special cake made for him with a picture of him and all of his boys. We also had baseball caps made with "I Am One of Sam's Boys" printed on the front. He was so happy to be with us and so happy to know we all loved him so much.

Letters Written by Muh Brown
(After Birthday Parties for Her in 1991 and 1993)

My Dear, Sweet Children,
I love you, I love you, and I thank you for adding sunshine to my birthday. If I looked the world over I couldn't find words large enough to thank you for all you did to make my birthday a

Birthday Parties In New Hill

happy one. It was so wonderful and you both are just little angels dropped from heaven.

You didn't look or act tired, but I know the bed felt good to you that night after cleaning up all the mess we left for you. If I am not around another year for my birthday, I want you to know you have made my life happy many, many times and I love you so much.

Someone who's so glad to share, so glad to help and give and care, adds something very special to the world. The two of you are just that.

Please excuse my writing. I hope you can read it. If you can't, just bring it over and I will read it to you. Ha! Just remember I am ninety-three years old. Again I want to say thanks again for everything. I love you so much.

—"Muh"

Bless Your Sweet Hearts:

I love you, I love you, and I thank you. Well, I have thought of words large enough to thank you for my wonderful birthday party, but I don't think anyone makes words large enough to express my thanks and love to you. So I will say I had such a wonderful, sweet, and precious time with my precious children. Peggy, you and Billy were so wonderful, going around loving everyone just like you were not tired and so happy and loving to everyone.

When I prayed last night I thanked the good Lord for you and asked him to bless you and give you long lives. I also prayed He would give all who came safe trips back home. Well, my dear children, I am going to let this do for this time. Thanks again and know you will always be dear to my heart.

I hope life brings you as much happiness as you have brought to me.

—"Muh"

P.S. Hope you can read this—just remember I am ninety-five years old now. Ha!

An Exceptional Journey

Muh Brown's Penny Poem
A big, silver dollar and a
Little brown cent
Rolling along together went
Rolling along on the smooth sidewalk

When the dollar said, for dollars do talk
You poor little cent
You cheap little mite
I'm bigger and twice as bright
I'm worth more than a hundred fold
And written on me in letters cold
Is motto drawn from the old creed
"In God We Trust," which all may read.

Yes, said the cent, I'm a cheap little mite
And I know I'm not big or shiny bright
But yet, said the cent, with a sweet little shy
You don't go to church as often as I.

FAREWELL "MUH"

She lay on her hospital bed too weak to speak. We leaned over to kiss her and tears fell from our eyes. We knew how sick she was but we could not bear to let her go. She had meant so much to us and to all of the children she had cared for over the years.

We told her how much we loved her and brushed her hair away from her face. She was like a little child, so helpless and small. Our hearts overflowed with sadness and love for this wonderful woman who had been a mother to so many.

Later in the day we received word she had passed on into the arms of her savior. We were both happy and sad for her. She had earned her place in heaven and we knew she was no longer suffering and was no longer in pain.

Her memory is so etched in our hearts that nothing will ever take it away. She was the angel you read about, but those of us who knew her lived with a real angel and we know she is looking over us now and making sure her children are OK. Farewell "Muh," you are the angel we loved and will never forget.

Raising Children And Working

Peggy

Billy was a really old-fashioned husband when it came to having his wife work outside of the home. He was OK with the brief period I worked for the television station but once Bruce was born, he wanted me at home, raising our two children. It wasn't easy for Billy because he wasn't earning a huge salary. He took a morning paper route to help us with our finances which meant he got up at four thirty each morning and delivered his papers. He later did some accounting for an automotive company. He was working three jobs but he had his wife at home with our children and that was the way he wanted it.

When Bruce, our youngest child, started kindergarten, Billy agreed I could go back to work part-time as long as I was at home when the children got out of school. I was happy because I couldn't imagine being at home each day by myself until the children returned from school. I immediately searched the paper for a position I felt I would be qualified for. I finally decided I would go to a temporary employment agency and get them to help me.

I accepted a position working only four hours per day. These hours were important because I needed to pick my children up from school in the afternoon. He agreed with the part-time hours and I went to work.

The agency was new and there was a lot introductory work such as typing invitations and letters. I worked for the agency for five years before it closed due to some legal problems. At the time the agency was located in an office building in downtown Raleigh. We had many job orders that had never been filled. I looked through them and saw an order for an administrative assistant for an architectural firm located in the same building on a different floor. I called and made an appointment to interview with them.

The appointment was for the coming Thursday. I went and interviewed with two architects who were still in their twenties. They were so cute and so smart. I was thirty-five years old. I was offered the job and I started on a Monday so I only missed one day of work. I absolutely loved working for the architects. It was a fun job and I got to do a lot of typing and bookkeeping. They were so talented and I just loved seeing them design huge buildings and major projects.

I worked for them on a part-time basis for five years. During that time Billy and I purchased a larger house with more than one bathroom. Life was good for us, and the children were doing well in school and enjoying sports activities. Even though things were going well for me and the children, many things were impacting Billy's life. The boss he admired and loved died of a sudden heart attack. For Billy it was like losing his father all over again. He could hardly believe it. The boss's son took over the company immediately. He was quite capable since he had grown up in the company and new all of its inner workings.

The son was young and, of course, made some decisions that were not the best. One was hiring a banker to be his right-hand man. This was the beginning of a nightmare for Billy, but he loved the company so much and could not imagine ever leaving. He had already put in almost thirty years, and he planned to stay until he retired. However this was not to be because the situation with the new management got to be more than he could handle.

I felt so bad for him. He had worked so hard to provide for us. I talked to him about my applying for a full-time job that would pay more and give him more options. I interviewed for a job with a large manufacturing company as a personnel assistant. I got the job and gave my resignation to the architects. I was sad to leave them but I needed to help Billy.

I was forty-one years old when I went to work at Exide Electronics on April 12, 1976. I spent my first few days in an older building that we would vacate in a few weeks. The company was constructing a new building to manufacture their products—uninterruptible power supplies. My office was a far cry from the beautiful office I had worked in with the architects. I was depressed and felt I had made a bad decision.

Billy was very supportive, as he always was, and told me I didn't have to work. He said he would take care of me. He had taken a new job, but his salary was less than what he had been making.

I persevered and began to enjoy my job. I particularly like working with hourly personnel. They were genuine and worked hard assembling products. I considered them the backbone of the company and loved interacting with them. I wanted so much to gain their trust and let them know I was an advocate for them and all employees who worked for the company. It took a while but I finally gained their trust and they became my best friends. I wanted to make sure they were treated fairly and with dignity. Human resources could make a big difference in how employees felt about the company.

I spent my days hiring new personnel and working with the employees on various issues they faced each day. I had new-hire orientation almost every day to introduce them to our benefits and give them some history of the company. Much of my time was spent on affirmative action issues as well as competitive pay structures.

I started receiving promotions within a year and pretty soon was part of management. I loved going to work every day and even though it was a thirty-five mile ride from home, it was worth it. I learned so much and was given the opportunity to continue learning the entire time I was employed by the company. I felt sad from time to time when one of our employees was seriously hurt or even killed. They were my family and I felt the loss. Each day there was something new and unexpected.

My last position was director of employee relations. Billy was so proud of me, he told everyone he talked to I was doing so well. I moved to the corporate offices to work with the salaried employees. It was a beautiful building and such a pretty place to work. However I missed the plant and the hourly employees.

The company was going through some acquisition changes and the new owners brought in their own CEO. Some of the vice presidents were laid off along with a number of salaried employees. We had to close a plant in Leland and lay off several hundred workers. It was a nerve-racking time and I will never forget it. I didn't know what would happen to me but I knew I would get a fairly decent severance package.

I prepared myself for the lay-off slip. It never came. One of the vice presidents who would be staying approached me and asked if I would like to work for him and go back to the plant. I was overjoyed. This vice president was a tough, hardworking gentleman but I didn't know for sure how he felt about me. I had worked with him on some personnel issues and did OK. I loved working for him because he was straightforward and honest. I always knew where I stood with him and he was quick to let me know when I had done a good job.

Shortly after moving back to the plant I was diagnosed with a voice problem called spasmodic dysphonia. This condition causes the voice box to shake involuntarily making me uneasy when doing presentations and speaking in front of anyone. I tried to hide it but the hourly employees knew me too well, and some asked me what was wrong with my voice. My secret was out, and I knew in my heart my career was over.

I went to my regular doctor and he said he couldn't detect any difference in my voice. I told him something was wrong. I later went to an ear, nose, and throat doctor and he did some tests and suggested I do an MRI. I called my regular doctor and told him what the ear, nose, and throat doctor had suggested.

He said, "I would like you to go to a neurologist first and get his opinion."

I did, that very afternoon. The neurologist asked me if I'd ever had an MRI and I told him I didn't know what it was. He then asked me if I was claustrophobic and I told him I was.

He said, "Then you'll probably want to take a valium before going into the tube."

He said I should do the MRI even though he saw no neurological issues with the brief test he performed on me. I scheduled the MRI and almost had a heart attack when I was placed in the tube. I had selected an open-air MRI thinking it would be better, but it wasn't. Unfortunately I didn't take the valium because I thought I would be fine in the open-ended machine. I got through it with the help of a valium drip.

The test showed nothing to identify my problem. My regular doctor consulted with some doctor friends of his and during their conversation they determined I had spasmodic dysphonia. I now had a diagnosis and did a little research on my own. I learned I had a very mild case compared to many others, but it was severe enough to keep me from performing my job. I was now sixty-four years old and decided to retire one year earlier than I had planned. Billy had already retired, and we could be together.

On June 10, 1999 I got dressed, kissed Billy goodbye, and drove the thirty-five miles to the company where I had so many friends I loved so much. Little did I know they had planned a huge retirement celebration for me. The event was held on company grounds, with a huge tent with banners and balloons to welcome the guests. There were chairs set up for hundreds of people. Right above the tent was a big sign that said "Peggy Griffin Day."

I was so overwhelmed as I walked toward the tent. All of the hourly workers were there to enjoy steak and all of the fixings. Employees had fans with my picture on the back and front. Chairs were lined up in front where management personnel would sit. Of course there were special seats for Billy and me. Management talked about my years with the company and my accomplishments. The hourly plant workers were given the opportunity to talk and I cried as I heard them acknowledge me in such kind ways. They spoke of the company Christmas parties we had attended and my visits to the hospital to see them when they were sick. They were so genuine and kind. I knew I had been accepted, and that was something I had strived for all my life. They were my family and I loved them just as if they were my children. They also gave me a crystal vase, jewelry, and flowers, many congratulation cards, and two big scrapbooks filled with pictures, letters, and other documents relating to my career.

Following the retirement celebration the human resources department held a private party in honor of my sixty-fourth birthday, which was on June 9. My coworkers gave me some outdoor furniture to use in my retirement, and the entire department enjoyed cake and ice cream. I will always love them and keep them close to my heart.

That day ended my working career, which I'd never expected or felt I deserved. I believe it was part of God's plan for me and I hope I did not disappoint Him.

* * *

Starting To Work

Billy

Billy's work life began when he was only seventeen years old. He relates his experiences:

There were several advantages to being an older boy at the orphanage. One was the opportunity to participate in the off-campus Diversified Occupational Work Program, which was designed to help the rising senior boys get acclimated to life outside of the orphanage. We each had a part-time morning job at a local business. The high school principal took me for an interview with a local wholesale distributor, the owner of which had previously hired two orphanage boys and been pleased with their performance. One of them had been drafted into the Army, but the other still worked there full-time, so the owner said he didn't need another worker. The principal convinced him he wouldn't be sorry if he gave me a chance. I went to work for the wholesale distributor and stayed there for more than thirty-five years.

I started on September 6, 1951. I worked from eight thirty to eleven thirty a.m. I had to be back on the orphanage campus by noon for lunch. At one o'clock school began and lasted until four. At four thirty I had practice for football, basketball, or baseball depending on which sport

Raising Children And Working

was in season. At six all 300 of us went to the main dining room for supper. Study hall was from seven o'clock until nine.

My first duties at my new workplace included running errands, doing maintenance around the office, helping with receiving, and stocking merchandise from our suppliers. At Christmastime I received a bonus of fifty dollars. Six months later the company relocated to a new building much closer to our campus. This cut down the time I spent walking back and forth to work and home again.

In June 1952 my boss called me into his office and offered me a full-time job to begin after my graduation from the Methodist Orphanage High School. I was put in charge of the warehouse and was responsible for receiving, stocking, and shipping all merchandise to our dealers in eastern North Carolina, which included fifty counties. As time went by I was promoted to different positions within the company.

Bob Warren, my first boss was like a second father to me, replacing the one I had lost when I was only eleven years old. He was a handsome, white-haired man; he was fit and had an air of quiet dignity about him. Mr. Warren had an extensive background in sports, but not many knew this as he didn't talk about himself. He was widely respected in the business world for his integrity, character, and honesty.

A former basketball player he had recruited while coaching at a local university said, "I never met a man quite like him. Mr. Warren was one of the most honest men I have ever seen and knew how to handle people." In fact one of my coworkers, who played football for him when he coached at our local university, said, "I've never met anyone who did not admire and respect him, and there's no estimating the impact he had on thousands of young people."

I was so in awe of this man, especially when I found out he'd been a fullback and linebacker on the NC State football team in 1927. They'd finished with nine wins and one loss. He'd also played guard on the 1929 basketball team that won NC State College's first Southern Conference title. A teammate once said, "He was a clean and tremendous competitor and was probably a better football player than he was a basketball player." Bob Warren never wore a helmet while playing, and he was a fierce linebacker. He blocked for a tailback who was named to the

All-American Football Team. You don't find a man like him often. Bob Warren never failed at anything.

In 1970 my boss had a sudden heart attack and died. I will always remember him. He taught me to give a full day's work for a full day's pay, how to treat people with dignity and respect, how to be a team player, and how to enjoy life. I will always be grateful to this man for having confidence in me and what he felt I could bring to his company.

I like to think he was proud of the contributions I made to the company he loved and founded. He mentored me and gave me a chance I wouldn't have had if he had not been so kind and compassionate.

After his death, his son, Bobby who was three years my junior, took control of the company. He was a smart, intelligent businessman and very capable of leading the company to success. Bobby had grown up with the company and learned his management style from his father. He also inherited some of his father's positive traits and had compassion for people and was kind to his employees.

I had deep respect for him until in my opinion he used poor judgment in hiring a general manager from outside the company. He told me about his plan and I was shocked. I knew the person he wanted to hire and I had no respect for him at all. I couldn't believe he would bring in a person with no experience in wholesale distribution to make decisions that would ultimately negatively affect the company.

After he told me this, I responded with what I believed he wanted to hear: "That will be fine." That was one of the worst mistakes I made in my lifetime. I have regretted it since. Being less than honest certainly changed my life and the company I loved and had worked for for so many years. I should have been more truthful, but it was not in my nature to speak negatively about anyone.

The character and integrity that had always been a part of the company seemed to slip away immediately after the new general manager came onboard. However I still loved and was loyal to the company, and I was determined to make sure it continued to thrive in every possible way.

In the wholesale distributing business, sales personnel are often given nice trips for their efforts. I wasn't in sales but was given the opportunity to go on a trip offered by a product manufacturer. Before

Raising Children And Working

Mr. Warren passed away, he called me into his office and told me he would give me a trip to Puerto Rico, and I would have the privilege of taking my wife with me. I was so excited to be going out of the country. Peggy and I had never flown in an airplane, and we had travelled no further than North Carolina. We would be gone for a week, which meant leaving our little girl, Brenda. Peggy's sister lived in a nearby town and offered to keep her for us. She had four boys and no girls, so she was delighted to have Brenda in her home even for a short time.

The trip was great except for one thing: Peggy got sick. We were told not to drink the water and we didn't, but Peggy did eat fresh fruit during a tour of the island. The natives were selling it on the side of the road. When all was said and done it was a trip to remember and one we will never forget.

A number of trips followed as my job offered more opportunities. We went to some really neat places. Bobby was generous, and he made it possible for Peggy to go on some of the trips with me. We went to Acapulco, Mexico; Honolulu and Maui, Hawaii; San Juan, Puerto Rico; Phoenix, Arizona; and Nassau in the Bahamas.

In 1971 I was name advertising and marketing manager of the company. In 1973, 1974, 1975, and 1976, the Zenith Radio Corporation awarded me certificates of merit for advertising and sales promotion activities. In 1977 it awarded me the National Advertising and Public Relationship Award. In 1981, after thirty years, I resigned and went to work for a restaurant equipment company. After three years there, I resigned to accept one of the most rewarding yet challenging positions I had ever had.

Around that time I received a phone call from Robert Kirkman, a gentleman Peggy and I had known for a number of years. He now owned a wholesale appliance distribution company. He asked me if I would be interested in going to work for him. I couldn't believe what I was hearing. God had surely answered my prayers. I knew I would be happy again in my work life.

After working for Mr. Kirkman for a year I became a sales manager; two years later I was president of the company. I bought stock in the company and Peggy and I took several trips offered to us by the company's product manufacturers. We went to Interlaken, Switzerland; Honolulu, Hawaii twice; Lake Tahoe, Nevada; Phoenix; Arizona, Rio de Janeiro, Brazil; and on a cruise to the Bahamas.

In December 1987, two of our manufacturers decided to make changes in the distribution of their products, forcing Mr. Kirkman to close the business to protect his retirement. This ended my employment with the company and my opportunity to own and manage my own company. It was devastating, but it didn't end my relationship with this person who believed in me and was willing to give me the chance of a lifetime. I will always admire and respect him. Peggy and I consider him one of our most treasured friends. It's not often that you're given the opportunity to work for a man of such extraordinary character. He was respectful and generous to all of his employees. He believed in sharing his good fortune with those who worked for him. He didn't give to himself more than he gave to each of his employees. He was a strong man and believed all people are important and deserve to be treated with respect. Peggy and I love him like a father.

Soon after the closing of the company, I received a much unexpected phone call from the wholesale distribution company where I had worked for more than thirty years. I was told they had a job for me and wanted me to come back. I was so shocked I was speechless for a minute. It didn't take me long to accept his kind offer.

On January 2, 1988 I went back to the first company I had ever worked for as a sales manager for one of the appliance divisions. I took the job on a smile and a handshake. Soon after returning I obtained for the company a high-end line of kitchen appliances, which we promoted in North Carolina, South Carolina, and Virginia.

After five years with the company, in May 1993, I was given the opportunity to go to work for a manufacturer out of California. This was something I had always wanted to do and I felt the opportunity would not present itself again in the future. I was successful in my sales efforts for the first two years of my employment, then I was diagnosed with cancer in 1994 and lost some momentum. Territories and sales objectives changed and I found myself struggling to make my quotas. I decided to retire in 1996 and look after my health. I also spent time working in my vegetable garden and walking with our dog, Lucy, in the woods of New Hill, North Carolina. It was very different but rewarding. I felt I had earned a long vacation from a work life that had its ups and downs. I had survived it all and felt good about my contribution to the business world.

Orphanage Alumni

Peggy

The most important people in the world to us, next to our biological families, are our brothers and sisters from the Methodist Orphanage. After all we spent our entire childhoods with them and they are very much a part of our lives. We loved it when those who had graduated came back for a reunion and stayed in the rooms of our building. We would give them our beds and we would sleep in the attic of the building. They always left us quarters or sometimes even fifty-cent pieces under our pillows when they left. For some of us, that was the only money we would have for the entire year. This was especially true when we were very young. Our biological families did not have money to give us, and we never expected it.

The weekend of the annual reunion was always exciting. There was a baseball game between the older alumni and those who still lived on the campus. It was fun to see the older alumni trying to show they were still in good shape and could beat their younger orphanage brothers. Billy remembers going to a reunion with his father and running the bases during the baseball game. He thought it was fun, but he never expected to live at the orphanage the same as his father had done.

An Exceptional Journey

After we graduated from the Methodist Orphanage High School and were married, we started to attend the reunions. It was so exciting to see everyone and to hear what they had been doing since leaving the orphanage. The reunion at that time was held on campus, in the gymnasium. We had lots of food and fellowship and attended church on Sunday.

Billy had always been a leader while living at the orphanage so it was no surprise when he was elected president of the alumni association. He was well respected and loved by everyone, and he welcomed the opportunity to lead the group. The reunion was a simple function until the 1990s, when Andy Kanas, a vivacious alumnus, decided we needed to kick it up a notch. He and a fellow alumnus contracted with a hotel to have our reunion convention style. This was a very risky move but Andy had made many risky moves and was now a successful restaurant owner.

Our first reunion held at a hotel was very successful. Those alumni who lived in other states felt the trip would be worth it to enjoy a first-class weekend. More than 200 alumni and their families attended. It was a fun-filled weekend, and a new trend was started.

Billy and I became involved by helping Andy with the reunion activities and when it was time to elect new officers, Billy was once again chosen as president of our association. He followed the format Andy had established and elaborated a little on the activities to make it more enjoyable. He served as president for two years, then another energetic alumnus took over: Bill Gilbert, an enthusiastic leader who created a lot of interest in the reunion. He was particularly adept at getting people to sing in the choir for our Sunday church service. He was somewhat of an accomplished musician and enjoyed using his talent.

The presidency changed back and forth between the three of them until, sadly, Andy had a fatal heart attack. It was devastating for the association, but we knew he wanted us to carry on with the reunions and make them better and better each year. During Bill Gilbert's last tenure as president he was diagnosed with cancer. He felt he could not serve again because of the stress of his treatments and he turned it over for the last time to Billy. Bill Gilbert lost his battle with cancer and died in 2004.

Billy retired in 1996 and I was planning my retirement in 1999. We discussed what we would do during our retirement years. We wanted it to be a time of service and commitment to a cause we really believed in. The more we discussed our plans the more we came back to working full-time to bring the alumni brothers and sisters together. We felt this could be done in several ways. We could continue to make the annual reunions better. We could do an annual breakfast where we would cook and serve to all who attended. We could continue with our annual picnic and make it fun and inviting. We could also do a semiannual newsletter and send it to everyone. We knew this was a lot but we felt we were up to the challenge.

We have kept our commitment to this day, and more than 200 alumni and their families continue to attend the reunions. We have added additional activities to the weekend such as bingo and a hospitality room to socialize and eat. We started a program to honor a past matron or teacher each year. We also recommitted our association to helping the Methodist Home for Children through our gifts and services. The Methodist Home for Children is all that is left of the Methodist Orphanage and they do a tremendous job of serving troubled youth and families. They have group homes and are a licensed adoption agency. They do tremendous work throughout the fifty-one counties in North Carolina. Recognizing those who played a major role in our lives while living at the orphanage is just one way we give back.

Our association supports the Methodist Home for Children with gifts and services. We support their scholarship and fundraising programs, and we contribute to an alumni endowment fund. On one occasion we got the names of children who needed gifts for Christmas. We collected so many gifts it took a truck to take them to the home where the children lived. We are proud to be associated with such a giving and loving group of alumni and their families.

At our annual Easter Reunion we have a packet for each alumnus containing an updated address book, an e-mail list, and a birthday list.

These lists encourage them to stay in touch with each other and visit when they know they are in a town or city where an alumnus lives.

Billy calls every alumnus in our address book on his or her birthday. We have more than 260 names listed, and each one gets a call. Some of them wait for his call; it's the only connection they have to their prior life. We have a list of 130 alumni we send e-mails to when there's a death or other news regarding an orphanage brother or sister. Most of our alumni are in their twilight years and do not have or use computers. Our newsletters list the deaths and also provide information regarding our activities throughout the year. Our orphanage brothers and sisters contribute stories for the newsletter and many of them include memories of their lives at the orphanage.

Many of our members are very generous in their financial support of our association. This makes it possible for us to do the things that keep us together. We have minimal dues that cover just a small portion of the cost of the weekend.

Billy and I are often asked how we do what we do for the association. It's a labor of love, and we couldn't do it without the help of so many orphanage brothers and sisters. We have a vice president and a treasurer who give their time and talents to help. We have people who cook for the breakfast and make baskets for the children at our Easter reunion. Some give raffle prizes and door prizes. Some donate stationery and printing. Many of our alumni give us extra money over and beyond their dues. Most of all they give us their love and support in everything we do.

Billy and I feel we are doing God's work by keeping our brothers and sisters together and making them happy.

Those of us who were raised in the Methodist Orphanage have a respect and love for the home where we were raised. We live with our memories every day, and we tell the stories to anyone who will listen. I can remember so many good times with my orphanage brothers and sisters, such as playing jack rocks in the basement of the Atwater Building or listening to *The Shadow* on the radio. I can remember playing scrub in the yard of our building and making a penny show for all to see. I can remember buying new clothes at Hudson Belk and dressing up to go to Sunday school at Edenton Street Methodist Church.

Orphanage Alumni

I remember May Day and dancing around the maypole, and I can remember Christmases at the orphanage. It was a magical time. I remember my best friends, including Martha. We climbed the large pecan trees on the rolling hills when we weren't supposed to. On one occasion she had climbed almost to the top when I felt limbs falling on me just below her. I thought she was throwing them, but soon I realized the sad truth: she was falling. I heard her hit the ground. She hollered that she was not hurt, but I saw blood in her mouth. She had bitten her tongue. I told her we needed to go to the infirmary. We decided we couldn't tell them we had been climbing trees, so we made up a story about falling over one of the concrete benches on the hills. I don't know if they believed us or not, but they treated her minor wound and we went back to planning our next adventure.

When Billy and I had the birthday parties for Muh Brown, we engaged a friend to cook the pig. He was unfamiliar with our orphanage family and said, "I have never seen a group of people like this. All of you seem to love each other so much and you show it without hesitation. There's so much hugging and laughing and you seem to be so close." Billy and I just smiled and told him we were a family that loved one another. We were no different from a normal biological family. There were just more of us.

When an alumni brother or sister is in the hospital, the orphanage brothers and sisters arrive to pay a visit. When they're told that only immediate family is allowed in, they reply very quickly that they are family. It's their sister or brother in there. On one occasion a nurse was overheard saying, "How many brothers and sisters does that man have?"

At a funeral of an orphanage brother or sister there are sometimes special rows of seats to accommodate the alumni who attend. Billy often gives the eulogy and tells the story of all our lives together and how much we mean to one another. After all there is no one who knows us better than our orphanage brothers and sisters.

We are hoping our annual reunions and other activities will continue for some time to come. This is unrealistic when you think of the ages of our alumni. Most of us are in our seventies and eighties. Five are in their nineties. It's getting more difficult for them to travel due to

An Exceptional Journey

health issues, so they have to stay home and let us inform them of how everything went by e-mail or newsletter. They never quit telling us how much they appreciate the birthday calls, newsletters, and e-mails. With this kind of love, how can we not do what we can to make them happy?

Have we chosen the right thing to do in our retirement years? I would say we have indeed. We will keep doing it as long as our health permits and as long as the orphanage brothers and sisters are able to get back to Raleigh for another great reunion.

However we don't always wait for the annual reunions to spend time with our orphanage brothers and sisters. On many occasions we get together in Calabash, where our orphanage sister Evelyn lives. Everyone who lives nearby or has a second home on the coast will travel to Evelyn's house and go to one of the local fish restaurants for lunch. Evelyn always has a delicious dessert for us to share when we return to her home after lunch. We sit and talk for hours, repeating the same stories over and over again. We are happiest when we are together.

Billy in Bunny Suit with orphanage brothers and sisters.

Fred Fletcher Park

Billy

When the orphanage was sold in 1984, all of the buildings were torn down with the exception of two: the Borden Building, the first building constructed on the campus, used as the superintendent's residence and later a cottage for boys ages seven and eight; and a new building that housed boys of sixteen to eighteen. A developer purchased part of the former campus and constructed condominiums. The City of Raleigh purchased twenty-one acres of beautiful, rolling hills and the two remaining buildings. It was a perfect setting for a park. The city even made plans to restore the Borden Building for weddings, meetings, gatherings, etc.

The alumni association decided we should have some kind of memorial in the park now owned by the city. Peggy and I agreed to meet with the director of Parks and Recreation to discuss the possibilities. It was not an easy task because the city did not generally allow this type of memorial within the parks throughout Raleigh. After a lot of talking, the director agreed to bring it before the Department of Recreation board of directors. Our proposal was overwhelmingly approved. The alumni would be responsible for any cost incurred for the memorial, and the city offered to help in any way possible. At our 1992 reunion our memorial was ready to be dedicated. It was beautiful. The inscription read:

> Dedicated to the Methodist Orphanage Alumni
> This twenty-one acre site is a portion of the original Methodist Orphanage, from 1899 to 1984. The Methodist Orphanage served the needs of children. The development of Fred Fletcher Park on this site perpetuates the memory of those children.

The dedication of the memorial featured Fred Fletcher, the gentleman for whom the park was named. The CEO of the Methodist Home for Children spoke, and the program highlighted the history of the Methodist Orphanage and what the home meant to so many children. It was a great day and all of the orphanage brothers and sisters were so proud.

The alumni raised more than $6,000 for the project. The memorial was designed by the city staff. It consisted of a block of granite about the size of a headstone surrounded by a semicircular seating wall. More than 200 azaleas, mondo grass, rhododendron, spirea, forsythia, hemlocks, pampas grass, and other plants surrounded the memorial. A group of thirty alumni, mostly in their sixties and seventies, planted all of the plants with the help of the city Parks and Grounds personnel.

The Raleigh Parks and Recreation Department's recognition of and involvement with the alumni was a positive and constructive effort. A portion of the place where the memorial is located has been restored to the rightful owners: the alumni of the Methodist Orphanage.

Peggy and I believe the park restored some measure of respect to the orphanage and the alumni, and the project has been one of our most rewarding endeavors. We are proud of the effort we put into bringing it to fruition. It has preserved a part of the beauty that is so much a part of Raleigh. When visiting the park, we can look out over the rolling hills and remember playing there, climbing the pecan and oak trees. The park is a tribute to the alumni who once lived at the orphanage.

The alumni decided to continue our efforts to get involved in Fred Fletcher Park. We began a project to raise money to help with the restoration of the Borden Building. It had fallen into disrepair and was in bad shape. The beautiful columns were damaged and several of the fireplaces had been almost destroyed.

Our alumni's gifts totaled $10,000. We presented a check to the Raleigh Parks and Recreation Department. For our generosity and interest, they dedicated one of the rooms in the Borden Building to the Methodist Orphanage/Methodist Home for Children Alumni Association. The room displays pictures of the orphanage family and other historical documents relating to the orphanage. The alumni association was given the first Fred Fletcher Award for our contribution to the park. We received this award at an awards ceremony held by the parks and recreation department.

METHODIST ORPHANAGE

Est. by Methodist Church, 1899; served children in central & eastern N.C. Campus here until 1979.

We were extremely honored when, on September 12, 2010, the State of North Carolina placed a historical marker on Glenwood Avenue in Raleigh, telling the story of the Methodist Orphanage. More than 165 alumni and family members attended the dedication. Raleigh Parks and Recreation supported us with tents and chairs so many alumni could attend. They made sure we had a sound system and even placed beautiful pots of flowers next to the podium. We served refreshments to all in attendance and made it a very special day.

After the dedication the alumni association treated all of the guests to a delicious barbecue lunch served in the administration building of the Methodist Home for Children. The historical marker stands proud and tall on the Fred Fletcher Park side of the property to tell everyone who passes that way that an orphanage once existed on the property and thousands of children were given a safe haven when there was nowhere else for them to go.

Just before the historical marker dedication, we visited the park and went to look at the memorial. We were saddened and amazed by how bad the area around the site looked. We talked to the director of Parks and Recreation and she said she would make sure that when all of the alumni and guests arrived for the dedication, the memorial would look better. She kept her word and those who had not seen the memorial were treated to a beautiful, clean area. One of our alumni donated beautiful pots of flowers to be placed around the memorial. Soon after the dedication, we decided to talk to the Parks and Recreation staff about maintaining the memorial area. Actually we had committed to keeping it up and had failed to do our part.

The volunteer services director for Raleigh Parks and Recreation Department suggested we replace the old and worn benches in the park. She said we could offer them to our alumni members and they could put plaques on the benches in honor or memory of people who are special to them. We accepted the challenge, but first we had to sign a volunteer contract with the city for one year. Peggy and I did this not knowing the full extent of how we would become involved in this project. We sent out a letter to our members explaining the project and we were astonished by the response we received.

In no time at all our alumni brothers and sisters purchased thirty-three benches. The city was so pleased and began the process of obtaining the benches. They are now spread out all over the park with beautiful plaques telling the stories of life at the orphanage and how much some

Fred Fletcher Park

of the people who lived there meant to all of us. Those who live in the condos across from the park are overjoyed by the new benches and are inspired by the history of the Methodist Orphanage.

This project went so well the city asked if we would consider refurbishing the picnic shelter in the park. We jumped at the chance to continue making our presence known on the campus where we once lived and played. They needed eight new tables, a grill, and two trash receptacles. Again we were shocked by the response from our brothers and sisters. In no time at all we had the tables purchased and installed. We even painted and stained the shelter to make it look like new.

In April 2010 we were surprised to learn we had been awarded the Fred Fletcher Park Volunteer award in recognition of our exemplary volunteer service to the City of Raleigh Parks and Recreation Department. The letter we received read: "You two have been selected to receive the outstanding adopt-a-park volunteer award. This award is given to only one person or couple during the year who volunteers for one of the city's thirty-three parks. It is one of the city's most coveted awards."

Peggy was in the hospital after having major surgery and was unable to attend the awards ceremony. Our daughter, Brenda, took her place and represented us proudly as she and her dad accepted the award.

History

In the latter half of the nineteenth century in North Carolina, people developed a great concern for the welfare of orphaned and dependent children. At the North Carolina Conference of the Methodist Episcopal Church in 1873, a resolution was passed to recognize the Orphan Asylum located in Oxford, North Carolina, as a worthy institution. The Oxford orphanage was established by the Masonic fraternity. The Protestant churches in North Carolina, in response to the need, developed orphanages, as did the Baptists, Presbyterians, and Episcopalians.

A committee made a resolution that each pastor in the conference would take up a collection for the Orphan Asylum in Oxford as a "collection for the poor." Many Methodists felt that to help other orphanages to care for orphans was not enough. They thought the Methodist Church had a responsibility that could only be met by creating its own orphanage. Reverend John Wesley Jenkins was a strong proponent of this idea. In 1898 the annual conference met and Rev. Jenkins proposed a committee be named to consider the establishment of an orphanage.

The committee started working immediately and decided to establish an orphanage in Raleigh. The first donation of one dollar came from Mr. W.W. Rose. Rev. Jenkins visited the president and secretary of the Chamber of Commerce in Raleigh, and they gave him some information on available sites around the capital city. The committee selected a forty-five acre plot in northwest Raleigh.

The orphanage committee applied to the general assembly for a charter, which was granted on March 6, 1889. The committee purchased the site for the orphanage for $ 3,800. The committee decided on a cottage plan with a large main building in the center for administration and educational purposes. Cottages could be added as needed to accommodate the growing institution. The Borden building, built in 1908, served as a home for Rev. Jenkins, his wife, and their children and remains on the former campus today.

The orphanage opened in 1901 to children of sound mind and body between six and twelve years of age. They were brought without any expense to the orphanage. They had to be recommended by their pastor, Sunday school superintendent, and one steward of the Methodist Church. On Thanksgiving Day, November 29, 1900, the first cottage was opened. The first child entered the orphanage on January 7, 1901. Her name was Cassie Bright. During that year twenty-eight children arrived at their new home.

The basement of the main building was used for cooking, dining, heating, storage, and bathrooms. The first floor housed the chapel, library, study, matron's rooms, and parlor. The second and third floors were for educational purposes.

The religious life of the children centered on the Brooklyn Methodist Church. They went to Sunday school and church there every Sunday. In the beginning the orphanage children went to city schools. In 1903 a teacher was hired and the orphanage school was started.

The activities of the children around 1904 were described by the superintendent as follows:

At half past five o'clock the rising bell would ring for the fire makers, and in a few moments they would go downstairs ready for duty. One little boy soon had a cheerful fire in the study hall ready for all to warm themselves when they came down from the dormitories. The kitchen boy, in the meantime, built his fire, and his cheerful whistle was heard as he took his lantern in hand and went out into the dark to the well for water. At six o'clock another bell rang and everybody arose, and in a short while the matron and two little girls joined the kitchen boy and all were busy getting breakfast.

As soon as it was light enough, the cowboys were off to their work, feeding and milking the cows. The horse boy was busy attending to the horse. The two room boys were in the dormitory sweeping and cleaning up. One of the large girls was left in the girl's dormitory to sweep, dust, and get the room in order. Two of the other girls were cleaning the halls, steps, and study hall. Five little girls looked after the porches and cleaned around the doors. The boys who had no special job before breakfast, if it were wash day, filled the tubs and boiler with water from the washerwoman.

At 7:15 a.m. breakfast was on the table and the warning bell was rung. The children got in line to enter into the dining room. The breakfast bell rang and all were expected to be in their places. The superintendent read the morning lesson from the Bible and said prayers, then one of the boys was called on to say the blessing. For twenty minutes everyone was busy and scarcely a voice was heard. Four little girls were kept busy waiting on the children. When breakfast was over everybody finished up their jobs and got ready for school.

At 8:15 a.m. all the children started out to walk one and a quarter miles to the city school. At 2:30 p.m. they returned and at 3:00 dinner was ready. After dinner the boys went out to do their work—some sawing wood, some cutting down trees, and others doing little jobs. If shoes needed mending our little cobbler got to work. The girls were engaged in all kinds of housework such as ironing, scrubbing, patching, darning, etc. A little sewing was done. Five little girls swept the yards.

At 5:00 p.m. all work stopped. The children frolicked and played until 6:00 p.m. At 6:30 supper was ready and the same religious services as at breakfast were held. At 7:00 study hour began. The smaller children retired at 8:00 p.m. and at 8:45 the larger ones went to their dormitories. By 9:00 all were in bed. The matron went around making sure all the children were comfortable and then she put out the lights. The day's work was done and the children slept soundly.

Rev. John Jenkins died on July 6, 1906. It has been said the orphanage was a great monument to Rev. Jenkins and was built through his energy and administration. He succeeded in founding and developing an institution that was a fountain of joy and a blessing to North Carolina Methodists in general, and particularly the orphan children. It was said Rev. Jenkins loved all little children and they loved him.

During the first year of his administration, the orphanage erected a new barn to care for the farming equipment. A steam laundry was built. Prior to his death, a movement to rebuild the Brooklyn Church was started in order to accommodate more adequately the children of the orphanage. The new church was dedicated as the Jenkins Memorial Church.

The trustees elected Rev. John N. Cole to succeed Rev. Jenkins as superintendent. He was well qualified for the position. He was recognized as a leader among the members of his conference and he served some of the larger churches of the North Carolina Conference. He had been a charter member of the board of trustees and had served in that capacity continuously from its beginning. He was familiar with the needs of orphan children for he had been an orphan in his boyhood, when he'd lived with some relatives in Oxford, North Carolina. He had a special love for children and tried to confer upon each child with whom he had any dealings the love he felt for his deceased son, who died at the age of thirteen.

He came into the administration of the orphanage with high ideals, which he expressed continually. The first task in an orphanage is to make a home for the homeless and to fill, as nearly as possible, the office of parenthood. It is hoped that every orphan child in his or her tender years shall have protection from an evil world. Surely it is the will of the Great Father that the orphan child, destitute of estate, shall be educated and trained for citizenship and for high purpose.

Rev. Cole's administration was marked by rapid growth and development. In 1911 the Page Building was erected as a residence for the boys and named in memory of A. Frank Page, the first large benefactor of the orphanage and a trustee in 1899. In 1913 the Jackson Building went up as a residence for girls in honor of Mrs. Mary J. Jackson. In 1914 water and sewer lines were installed and connected to the City of Raleigh systems. A steam laundry was built. Enrollment reached 166 students and five officers and teachers.

Rev. Cole died on January 1, 1915 and it was said he had found his higher purpose at the orphanage. All the children loved him with the closest affection and called him Father. His work at the orphanage was his most enduring moment.

So it could be justly said Rev. Cole brought to the administration of the orphanage the full experience of his life as a minister of the gospel. It was there he found the best possible field for his sympathy to invest itself. He brought to play upon the institution his fine judgment as a businessman and built securely upon the strong foundation already laid, making friends by the hundred for this home so sacred to our people.

Rev. A.S. Barnes was elected to succeed Rev. Cole on January 21, 1915. It seemed fitting since the association between the two men had been so intimate. Rev. Barnes had made the decision to enter the ministry while Cole was his pastor, and Cole had remained his spiritual advisor throughout the years. Rev. Barnes reiterated continually in his messages to the official board of the orphanage that an orphanage ought to have one great outstanding object in view in the training of the children committed to its care. Surely moneymaking should not be the dominant purpose. It should be the policy of those in charge to run it as economically as possible. He always bore in mind the children should have good, wholesome foods, comfortable clothes, and the best school advantages.

Children of a young, tender age should not be dwarfed physically by exacting of them hard work in order to make money. In fact an orphanage should not be considered a moneymaking institution but a character-making one. Children of mature years should be taught to accomplish everything that has to be done about the home and farm. They are to be fitted physically, mentally, and spiritually to assume the responsibilities that await them when they arrive at manhood and womanhood.

In the orphanage school, there were four teachers each in charge of two grades, totaling eight grades. A teacher taught one grade in the morning and one in the afternoon. The courses of study corresponded with those taught in city schools. Rev. Barnes had ideals of maintaining economy, making the orphanage a cooperative enterprise and producing Christian lives. He maintained high requirements the employees and workers were to meet including good health, education, cooperative spirit, and understanding of children.

During his administration the number of teachers increased from fifteen to twenty-eight. In 1915 his salary was $2,000—a big increase since the opening of the orphanage, when Rev. Jenkins received $900. Throughout the years Rev. Barnes kept aware of the progress of every child at the home and those who had graduated. The orphanage developed a remarkable record in preventing delinquency. He did resort to a dismissal if a child had a bad influence on the orphanage. The peak of enrollment reached 340 in 1931. In 1928 children were permitted to enter the orphanage at the age of two and a half years. In 1919 the trustees decided to allow the children to remain in the orphanage beyond eighteen years old.

It was the intention of the administration to save space for children whose parents were both dead, but in some extreme cases children were admitted even if their parents were living. Children were dismissed prior to the customary age of eighteen if their mother or relative became financially able to take care of them, if they developed any mental disorders, or if they could not maintain the standard of discipline.

On February 13, 1917, the Number One cottage was destroyed by fire. In 1918 an infirmary was built. In 1919 the first class graduated from the Methodist Orphanage High School. In 1924 the Administration Building was built to replace the old Number One building. A dining hall, the Atwater Building, a residence for girls, and a swimming pool were built. In 1927 the Baby Cottage, intended for the care of preschool-age children, was built. In 1930 a new home for the superintendent was built and the old one was remodeled into a residence for boys. All farming operations were moved to the Caraleigh farm, south of the campus.

History

In 1932, the orphanage school entered the state school system, which made it a unit of the Raleigh Public School System. Some of the boys were trained in farming, dairying, trucking, running machinery, carpentry, and plumbing. The girls were trained in housekeeping, sewing, laundering, cooking, serving meals for small children, and caring for small children. In 1938 the Burwell Building, a residence for older girls, was built. A central Steam plant was built to serve the dining room, administrative building and laundry for heating purposes. In 1940 a gymnasium was constructed along with an athletic field and three tennis courts.

This is a copy of a letter written by Superintendent Albert S. Barnes and sent to all mothers, fathers, and relatives of the children of the Methodist Orphanage on January 12, 1943:

I am addressing this form letter to all fathers, mother's relatives, and friends of our children with the hope and prayer you will read it carefully and prayerfully. I am outlining plans that, if accepted and carried out, will be of tremendous service to our children and to you. Following are some of the plans I have in mind for your thoughtful consideration.

1. When writing to any of our children or visiting them, please do not write or tell them anything that will upset or sadden them, but always write cheerful letters or tell them you are glad and happy for them to be here in the home.

2. Urge the children to study hard, make good grades, and obey the few simple rules that are laid down for their good.

3. Some of the relatives of our children come to see them too often and want to take them out of school or away from their work and the duties that have been assigned to them. When that is done it retards the children in school and disrupts their work programs.

4. During the last year or two I have had many requests for children to visit their relatives during the school term. If I let a few go, other mothers think their children should go also, and that creates a great deal of dissatisfaction and resentment on the part of all the other children when they cannot go too. It is my desire and purpose to treat the relatives of all children as nearly alike as possible. What is done for one child, all the others feel should be done for them as well. I am sure you understand and appreciate this earnest request.

5. It is not the policy of the board of trustees of the Methodist Orphanage to return children to their mothers and relatives after they have been in the home for several years. The reason for that policy is that we need the middle-sized and large boys and girls to help care for the smaller and helpless. It is costing the Methodist Orphanage $400 per year for every child in the home, and the trustees do not feel—after they have put $1,500 to $3,000 or $4,000 into the support and training of a child—that children should leave the orphanage before they graduate from our high school. This summer I have twenty to twenty-five requests from relatives of our children to return them to their people, which have caused a great deal of restlessness, discontent, and resentment. In such cases the children become very unhappy and feel the orphanage is doing them an injustice. This attitude on the part of some of the relatives of our children has made our work very difficult and is hard to combat successfully.

6. The children in the Methodist Orphanage get three square, wholesome meals every day, lovely cottages in which to live, serviceable clothes for working, and beautiful clothes to wear on Sundays and special occasions. The orphanage can justly boast of one of the best schools in the state for our children. We have many facilities for their recreation and play, and one of the best things about our orphanage is that it gives security against future want and prepares the children to become self-supporting after

they have finished at our orphanage school. I think it is very unwise for the relatives of our children to ask them to give up their security and future success for insecurity and possible future failure. I feel sure you appreciate the wonderful advantages our children have and enjoy here at the Methodist Orphanage.

7. There is another important matter to which I want to call to your attention. Most of our children have entirely too much spending money to throw away. I am glad for them to have a little spending money for their pleasure, but it is a shame for them to squander as much as they throw away each year. As stated above it is costing the Methodist Orphanage $400 for every child in the home, and some mothers and relatives send me monthly contributions to help support and maintain their children while they are in the home, which is most commendable. Since the orphanage has relieved many mothers and relatives of the financial care of their children, I think it just and proper that they should make sacrifices for their children by sending reasonable amounts of money to the orphanage each month for their upkeep. I am suggesting and asking all who can do so to make personal sacrifices, to share with the Methodist Orphanage some of its heavy financial obligations. It is costing us this year more than $125,000 to maintain and operate our home. I trust you see the reasonableness of this request to send me as much money as you can spare each month to help support your own children and relatives. I am well aware of the fact that there are some mothers and relatives so situated that they cannot make monthly contributions to the orphanage for the purpose I have mentioned. I do hope that all who can will comply with this request.

8. The Methodist Orphanage is endeavoring to protect and safeguard its children from many of the snares and pitfalls into which so many young people are falling. Recently it was announced in the papers of the state that there were at least sixty

babies born in Wake County out of wedlock, and that it is a true picture of what is happening all over this state and country. Frequently I receive letters from brokenhearted girls, asking the Methodist Orphanage to take their babies born out of wedlock. Our children are protected from the temptations to which so many girls are subjected. We are not only trying to teach our girls to be pure and virtuous, but we are also trying to teach our boys to be clean and pure, as well as our girls. Sin and crime are rampant everywhere, and I feel confident that you know these things too, and that you want to do all within your power to keep your children pure and clean and free from such loose living.

9. I want to take advantage of this opportunity to thank mothers and relatives who have been and are cooperating with me and my staff of workers in their sincere efforts on behalf of all our children. As I said in the beginning, this is a form letter, and what I have said does not apply to all the mothers and relatives of our children, but it does apply to a great many to some degree.

Trusting and praying that you will accept this form letter in the spirit in which it is written and that you will do everything in your power to help us in our difficult and arduous undertaking to train and develop our children into beautiful and worthwhile Christian characters, and with sincere good withes for you always, I am
Yours cordially; A. S. Barnes

P.S. I am very sorry the Methodist Orphanage is not prepared to furnish meals and rooms to visitors. A.S .B

The activities of the orphanage were arranged to enable the children to achieve the greatest benefit from their participation. The day began at six o'clock each morning. A bell sounded for everyone to get out of bed and eat breakfast at six thirty. The first through eighth grades attended classes in the morning and worked during the afternoon. The ninth through twelfth-grade classes worked in the morning and went to school in the afternoon. Recreational and leisure time occurred intermittently throughout the day. Three meals were served daily in the dining hall. The meals were all prepared by the students.

The program of work activities was under the supervision of competent leaders. Assignments were made on a rotating basis so all children had the opportunity to gain some experience in many projects. Work activities for girls included preparing food, laundry, sewing, housekeeping, caring for smaller children, and library work. Twelve girls worked in the kitchen. Six cooked the vegetables, two prepared breads and desserts, and the others cooked the meats and cleaned the kitchen.

Eighteen girls did the laundry work. One operated the tubs; another operated the wringers; and other girls pressed and ironed. These girls did all the laundry for the orphanage. The sewing room where seven girls repaired and renovated clothing was located above the laundry. Seven other girls took care of smaller children. Two girls assisted in library work. Twenty-seven girls did general housework in the various girl's cottages. The boys participated in farming, dairying, maintenance and repair, housework, school workshop, barbering, and some vocational training.

The library contained 2,612 volumes arranged in decimal classification. There was a card catalogue and a loan system. The children visited museums, libraries, social service agencies, courthouses, etc. The school had science clubs, a newspaper, glee clubs, dramatic clubs, debating clubs, etc.

Each cottage had a game room. There were also outdoor playgrounds. The children played ball games, marbles, and other games that normal children play. The orphanage sponsors organized football, basketball, baseball, and softball teams.

The children were allowed to attend the movies through the courtesy of the theater management. A monthly dinner was given for all children who had birthdays in the given month.

An Exceptional Journey

This was all possible under the direction of the Reverend Albert Sidney Barnes, superintendent from 1915 to 1948. All the children became to know him as Daddy Barnes. His mission statement was:

It is the product we send out into the world that is to determine our success or our failure. We want a homelike atmosphere to prevail. It is our constant endeavor to keep high ideals of life before those committed to our keeping. To fill these young lives with a holy ambition to be and to achieve is a task we resolutely set ourselves to accomplish. If we succeed in sending out into the world young people physically fit, mentally trained, socially adjusted, and spiritually minded with a purpose to render society worthwhile service, our ambition and dreams will be realized in a very large measure.

Peggy with Daddy Barnes on our wedding day.

Memories

When you have had the privilege of being raised with over three hundred brothers and sisters there are always many memories—not only yours but of those you lived with over the years. Below are some of the notes and articles written by alumni and shared with us.

A LOVE STORY

On June 8, 1931, I took that long ride from Glenwood Avenue to the Vann Building. I saw cows grazing on the hills. My first cottage was the Borden Building. I learned to love peanut butter and zip (molasses). I enjoyed living with thirty-five boys. We learned to play together. Sometimes we had a few fights that we soon forgot. I moved to the Brown Building with "Muh" Brown and that was a pleasant experience.

I enjoyed the private school and I loved to read. Miss Mary Ferree opened the world of learning to me. Miss Mary was like an angel. I loved her very much. She sent me into the future for further education with few pitfalls. I thank my Lord every day for having her as my teacher.

I moved to the Page Building and then to the Cole Building. I had various duties including some on the Caraleigh farm. I learned to milk cows and that was a unique experience. Driving a two-mule plow taught me patience. During my last two years at the orphanage I was given the job of taking care of the boiler room below the kitchen. This was a joy beyond my wildest imagination.

Some day I may write a book about the positive side of being in the orphanage, since I have read the bad side as written by others. It would seem they were not at the same Methodist Orphanage I was. My brother was adopted and lived in the country. I was approached about being adopted. This would have meant I would have gone to live on a farm. I quickly told them I was perfectly happy living at the orphanage. I did not want any part of the tobacco fields, sleeping on hay beds, using outdoor toilets, being cold at night, and not having the relationships I had with all my newfound brothers and sisters.

I thank my Lord for sending me to spend eleven years at the Methodist Orphanage. They were the best years of my life.

—Grady

CLARA'S PRECIOUS MEMORY

Looking back, some or most of my memories are the same as all the other brothers and sisters I lived with at the Methodist Orphanage. One of my first memories stands out to me. I'm sure some of the older group remembers how Daddy Barnes would let us play after chapel services in front of the main buildings. When we were ten years old Ed Williams would chase me and untie the ribbon in my hair. I thought he was a pest until one night he brought me a piece of penny candy. From then on he had my attention. There were smiles and waves across campus, notes (I still have two of them), and lots of hidden glances at each other.

As Ed and I grew, we found time to see each other every chance we had, and yes, we had those communal dates at the Burwell Building under the matron's watchful eye. We both left the orphanage in 1940, and in 1943 we were married. Ed and I were blessed with fifty-six years together.

Love is my memory of the home: love of God, love of family and friends, and the love of my life—Ed.

—Clara

I REMEMBER

There are quite a few stories in my memory of the time I was a student at the Methodist Orphanage in Raleigh during the early part of the century. But the one I am going to tell is unique.

Each September our student duties were changed, and we kept the chore we were assigned until the following September. During one chore period out of the many I had, I was mending shoes—I worked half a day and my friend John would work the other half. While we worked in the shoe shop, we got an empty molasses barrel from the pantry. We then went searching for locust pods and ripe persimmons. We baked several sweet potatoes, broke up the pods, mashed the persimmons, added sugar and water, sat back, and let it ferment.

After several weeks we were drinking the beer we had brewed. One day the superintendent suddenly walked in and demanded to know what we were drinking. We informed him and he too partook—without comment. After his departure we discussed our forms of punishment. We concluded we were going to get the axe. Much to our surprise, nothing was ever said.

However, the superintendent sent his office girl with an empty pitcher each night while we were in study hall so I could fill it with the home brew. This went on for quite a few nights until the barrel was empty. No more brew. Boo hoo.

—Bruce

An Exceptional Journey

FOR THESE AND ALL THY GIFTS OF LOVE
WE GIVE THEE THANKS AND PRAISE.
Lord, it wasn't so long ago in a place they call MO
Where the boys and the girls were running free
Preacher Barnes standing there teaching us a simple prayer
When they rang the dinner bell for you and me
I can still hear him say, "Let's all bow our heads and pray
Thank the Lord for His blessings every day"
Jus a simple little prayer, all the boys and girls were there
"For these and all thy gifts of love, we give thee thanks and praise"
Now today, when I'm alone, I keep thinking of a home
Where they rang the dinner bell and said a prayer
All the love and memories, they keep coming back to me
And I thank my lucky stars that I was there.
—Henry

Memories

Wedding day.

We Hold Hands And Walk Together

It is a slightly windy day at Kure Beach and we are getting ready to go for our afternoon walk. We put on our jackets and go down the steps from our beach house leading to the driveway. Just as we get to the street, Billy takes my hand and we begin our walk around the circle of our neighborhood. We always do this before we leave the area for adjacent neighborhoods.

There are other people walking their dogs and some couples walking for exercise. Everyone speaks even though we have never met. That is the way it is in the south. Being friendly is just the way we are, and wishing your neighbor a good day is our way of saying we like you.

The postmistress drives by in her car and hollers out the window, "You two lovebirds are still holding hands." Another guy walking by says to us, "You two must like each other."

He's right—we do like each other, and walking while holding hands is something we have been doing since 1950. The first time Billy and I were together as a couple, he took my hand and walked with me to my building on the orphanage campus.

We've been through good times and hard times, but through it all our love has been our strength. We've held on to each other when we've been sad and we hold on to each other when we are afraid. We're one in every sense of the word, and now that we're in our twilight years we take each precious moment we're together and we make it last as long as we can.

We're so truly blessed. We have a loving family and we have beautiful places to spend our time together. We have friends who are forever loyal, and we have our orphanage family. We have our work with the alumni association and we are gratified when we hear from orphanage brothers or sisters thanking us for loving them. We will go on doing what we can to keep us together as long as we can. We know the work we do is for a good cause and we know it is appreciated, and that is the best gift of all.

Tomorrow is another day. We will get up early and have our coffee and then Billy will make his birthday calls to his orphanage brothers and sisters. When afternoon comes we will once again go for our walk and yes, we will be holding hands. That is what we do and we will keep on holding hands until death do us part.

* * *

We have walked many paths together over the years. We walked to find time alone to discuss our workdays, our family concerns, our orphanage brothers and sisters, and many other subjects. We walked to enjoy the beauty of nature; the birds singing is comfort to our hearts and gives us cause to rejoice in God's creation.

As partners we have walked life's pathways side by side through many trials and rough patches. Depending on the circumstances, one of us has taken the lead and provided a helping hand of encouragement and strength. We learned that sometimes we can walk side by side and other times we walk in single file. One of us reaches back with a steady hand, and both of us cling to each other.

Sometimes life is slippery like ice. While we cannot always make the danger go away we support each other through the treacherous passages. Life is better and safer when it's shared with someone who cares for you and for whom you care. Life is better together.

I cannot begin to express the happiness that has come to me since Peggy became a part of my life. I am confident this was God's plan. Who would ever believe two people who both lost their fathers at an early age would become one? The love we have for each other gets stronger as each day passes.

There are hundreds of stories I could tell about the Methodist Orphanage, but the most important one is why I was there in the first place. Although it was not my decision to make the orphanage my home for more than six years, my life changed the day my brother and I entered the orphanage and I met Peggy.

The orphanage became the home I would love. I learned many things, made many friends, had new brothers and sisters, and grew both morally and spiritually. I came to revere the orphanage as a place that sheltered me, fed me, and nurtured me. I will carry the values I learned there as long as I live.

For me the orphanage was not just a place to live and grow. It was where I played my first real baseball game, my first football game, and my first basketball game. It was where I had my first fist fight and learned to lose. It was also where I learned to win with dignity and humility. It was where I met my life partner, Peggy. We have now been married for fifty-seven years. Together we raised two wonderful children and enjoy five grandchildren and three great-grandchildren.

I am asked from time to time to speak to high school students about growing up in an orphanage. The first thing I ask them is, "What comes to your mind when you hear the word *orphanage*?"

They say "Orphan Annie," "sadness," "poor people," or "not being with family." Well, they're all wrong about the orphanage where I was raised. I was certainly considered an orphan because I had lost my father at an early age. But I was probably better off than most boys and girls because I had a roof over my head, a warm bed to sleep in, and three meals a day. I had a better chance at life by growing up in this place.

We continue to love the place that was there for us. We continue to love every brother and sister who lived there with us and was a part of our very large family. No, it was not my decision to live at the Methodist Orphanage, but I sure am glad my mother made the decision for me because I had a good life and have always been grateful for the home that made room for me when I had nowhere else to go.

I am also thankful the Methodist Orphanage was a home for my wife Peggy (nee Patton); my brother, Donald Griffin; my father, Ray Griffin; my uncle, Hugh Griffin; my aunt, Della Lee (Griffin) Yates; my aunt Georgia (nee Griffin); my aunt Kathleen (Griffin) Mason; my cousins Alice (Mason) Warner, Ann (Mason) Oosterhoudt, and Buddy Mason; my great-uncles Jasper Dickinson and Don Dickinson; my brothers-in-law Joe Britt, KC Patton, Orlando Patton, and Sam Ellis; and my sister-in-law, Ann (Patton) Ellis.

Epilogue

Peggy

After graduating from high school, our daughter Brenda attended North Carolina State University and later transferred to Appalachian State University, where she received her degree in elementary education. She has enjoyed a career directing a preschool. Her love for children has motivated her to be involved in preschool curricula for more than twenty-five years. She believes—and we do too—that this is her purpose in life and she has fulfilled it well. We are very proud of her.

Brenda married John Holladay in 1980 and they have blessed us with three wonderful grandchildren—Justin, Daniel, and Stacey. John is a wonderful man who lives by his faith, and we are so proud to have him as our son-in-law. We have enjoyed being a part of their lives. Our oldest grandson, Justin, and his beautiful wife, Crystal, have blessed us with three beautiful great-granddaughters—Caroline, Campbell, and Kennedy. Our granddaughter Stacey married Jonathan Lee in April of 2011. He is an exceptional young man and we are proud to have him as part of our family. Our grandson Daniel continues to make us proud with his extraordinary accomplishments in school and his working career.

After graduating from high school, Bruce studied at North Carolina State University. He later received a degree in business from North Carolina Wesleyan College. He graduated with honors and is now executive director of a YMCA in West Chester, Pennsylvania. He started his career with the YMCA as a swim coach. He was an excellent coach and made life friendships with many of his swimmers. He always loved the YMCA and enjoys making a difference in the lives of many young people.

Bruce has blessed us with two wonderful grandsons, Connor and Bryce. He married Meredith Lewis in 2001. She is a talented and lovely woman and we are so proud to have her as our daughter-in-law. We enjoy the holidays with them and see them whenever we can. Bruce's oldest son, Connor, is following in his father's footsteps: he is an assistant swim coach for a YMCA team in Greensboro, North Carolina. His son Bryce has recently graduated from high school and is attending a community college in Greensboro, N. C.

We are proud of our children and grandchildren and know that whatever they decide to do in life, they will do it with integrity and honor. They are kind and considerate of others and have made us proud with the choices they have made. They have dealt with adversities and become stronger, and they continue to live their lives with hope and joy in their hearts.